ALSO BY PHILIP GONZALEZ AND LEONORE FLEISCHER

The Dog Who Rescues Cats

THE BLESSING OF THE ANIMALS

TRUE STORIES OF GINNY,
THE DOG WHO RESCUES CATS

PHILIP GONZALEZ AND **LEONORE FLEISCHER**

PHOTOGRAPHS BY JOAN BARON

HarperPerennial

A Division of HarperCollinsPublishers

First HarperPerennial edition published 1997.

Designed by Gloria Adelson
Photographs © 1996 by Joan Baron

The Library of Congress has catalogued the hardcover edition as follows:

Gonzalez, Philip, 1932–
    The blessing of the animals : more true stories of Ginny, the dog who rescues cats / Philip Gonzalez and Lenore Fleischer. — 1st ed.
        p.   cm.
    ISBN 0-06-018686-0
    1. Dogs—New York—Long Beach—Biography. 2. Cats—New York—Long Beach—Biography. 3. Gonzalez, Philip, 1932– . I. Fleischer, Leonore. II. Title.
SF426.2G658   1996
818' .5403—dc20   96-22047

ISBN 0-06-092867-0 (pbk.)

97 98 99 00 01 ❖/RRD 10 9 8 7 6 5 4 3 2 1

To King Solomon, Chairman One, and Lulu—Ginny and I will meet you all again someday at Rainbow Bridge.

—Philip Gonzalez

My share in this book is dedicated to the memory of Sedgewick and Edith, two wonderful cats I recall with great affection. And, of course, to my blessed Mitzi Thugater Fleischer, who, after seventeen short years of perfect felicity, still makes me melt at the sight of her pink candy nose, her black velvet ears, and her golden-eyed smile.

—Leonore Fleischer

Contents

ACKNOWLEDGMENTS

Ginny's and Philip's grateful thanks to:

Phyllis Levy, who believes in Ginny.

Larry Ashmead, our editor, who knew that people wanted to read more of the adventures of The Dog Who Rescues Cats.

Jason Kaufman, Marshall Trow, Krista Nordgren, and all our other good friends at HarperCollins who helped and supported us.

Cleveland Amory and Tiger Bear.

Authority cat and dog food, Iams cat and dog food, Petland Discounts, and Irene of American Eagle Foods, for their donations of nourishing food to our hungry outside cats.

Joan Baron for her wonderful photographs.

Kim Buckley and Don Quilfoil of Pet Supplies Plus of West Hempstead, NY for their generous donations of cat food and litter.

The Airtite Window Factory in Long Beach for letting us feed the strays on their property.

Ken Colon, Joe Palazzo, and James Hodge of the Long Beach Animal Shelter for their continued kindness to animals.

Jackie and Janet of PAWS (Pets Are Worth Saving) of Hicksville, New York.

The veterinarians and staff of All Creatures for their many hours of care.

Carol Weinstein, Ginny's attorney, for her donations of money and, more important, her time.

The Reverend William H. Pindar of the Central Presbyterian Church for honoring us at the Blessing of the Animals.

Dr. Angelica Petrides, who brought us Rainbow Bridge.

Bill Edwards of Barnes & Noble for his encouragement and support.

Emanuel and Naomi Diraclles and Peter Kerrigan for chauffeuring Ginny in style.

Dawn Hernandez of Warner Bros. Records.

All the teachers and wonderful children who welcomed Ginny and me into their classrooms and listened to her story with so much interest.

Dawn and Tara Coombes for their support.

Rebecca Beard for her support.

Diane Bell for the numerous good things she has done for us.

Ruby Leivent for her invaluable help with my correspondence.

Pat Ceratano, Norman Hunter, and Marilyn and Arthur Gales.

Long Beach City Manager Edwin L. Eaton.

Angela Toomey, Doc Perrins, and all members of the Long Beach Humane Society.

Art Ackerman of the Long Island Cat Fanciers Association.

The hundreds of people who took time to write letters to Ginny and me, and who sent in money to feed the cats. We haven't the space to list you all, but you know who you are, and you include: Maxine Beige, Georgia Hughes, Charles Northrop, Charlie Falco, Ileana Negron, M. Teri Scherer, Janice Ingram, Mary Judy Aloia, Lauren O. Risoli, Timothy Murray, and so many more.

Last, but of course never, never least, a million thanks to Ginny's "mommy" Sheilah, who's now more into cat rescue than ever, and who is more dependable than the Post Office in rain, snow, heat, and gloom of night in getting food to our street cats twice a day, every day.

CHAPTER 1

THE BLESSING OF THE ANIMALS

*C*HRISTMAS EVE, 1995. Earlier in the week we'd had some snow, and there were still white patches sticking to the ground, but this evening gave us the gift of a clear, bright heaven filled with stars. Chilly, maybe, but what else do you expect in New York City at the end of December? By five o'clock in the afternoon it's already dark, and early evening seems to be a lot later. But Christmas Eve is such a special time of the year that even the dark heavens are brighter, and the city streetlights appear to be wearing halos. There's something wonderful about a big city in the Christmas season; it feels a lot more peaceful at that time than during the other weeks of the year.

My dog Ginny, my friend and fellow cat rescuer Sheilah Harris, and I had been invited by the Reverend William H. Pindar to appear as his special guests at the Christmas Eve Blessing of the Animals held in the Central Presbyterian Church on Park Avenue and Sixty-fourth Street. Of course we said yes. It was too great an honor to pass up, and we were eager to participate because we'd heard so much about it.

All the way into Manhattan from Long Beach we were excited and on a high. A wonderful thing had happened that very day—not just one but three of our rescued homeless cats had been adopted into good homes just in time for Christmas. They had been waiting in our veterinarian's office for some kind person to take them in and give them a new life. What better time than Christmas Eve?

The Blessing of the Animals is a yearly event, much loved and heavily attended, when people come from far and wide to bring their pets to the church for a Christmas Eve service and a special blessing. Ginny and I were asked to take part in it because our friend Phyllis Levy is also a good friend of the pastor, and because I had written a book about Ginny's amazing adventures in saving the lives of homeless and disabled cats, *The Dog Who Rescues Cats*. Thanks to the book and to the publicity that came out of it, my Ginny was now a celebrity. More and more people were finding out about her miraculous rescues.

Ginny and I, along with my best pal Sheilah Harris, arrived at the church with Sheilah carrying the Chairman, a remarkable little cat I'll tell you more about later. There we met up with Phyllis Levy, her mother, Ruth Jaffe, and author Cleveland Amory, who's been a good friend to Ginny and me, and whose books I have always admired. Cleveland's work in animal rescue is a legend. Joining us also were Phyllis Levy's good friends Marion Finger with Schatzi, her schnauzer, and Amy Lemel with her Maltese Ovvy. Our little group was seated in the two rows down front, almost directly in front of the communion table.

I looked around me; this was not the first time I'd been to a service in a church that wasn't a Roman Catholic church, but places of worship have always held an interest for me. I'm a spiritual person who always feels close to God in the temple of any religion. I've visited a number of synagogues and churches of different denominations. When I was stationed in Vietnam, I even went to a Buddhist temple. But the church I'm most familiar with is the Catholic church of my childhood, which I attended frequently as a boy.

The Central Presbyterian Church is an awe-inspiring and majestic structure with high vaulted ceilings, large and colorful stained-glass windows, and the handsome carved cross hanging above the communion table. The communion table itself was banked high with fresh Christmas greenery—fragrant branches of pine and balsam—and flowers. Many pots of red and white poinsettias were in full bloom, and tall white candles burned brightly. Every candle was lit except one, the tallest, which rose high above the others.

The differences between my boyhood church and the Central Presbyterian Church were fascinating to me as I looked around. For one thing, there was no familiar altar, which in my church was high and richly adorned. Instead of an elaborate altar, there was a simple communion table. For another, the cross above the communion table had no figure of Christ hanging on it. The cross was beautifully made, but simply carved. I didn't see any statues of the Virgin Mary or the saints, as there are in Catholic churches. Yet all churches are sanctified places, and this one thrilled me to my heart.

Ginny's nose twitched at all the new odors that were teasing her—the evergreens, the polished wood of the paneling and pews, the sweet honeyed beeswax of the candles, the perfumes the women parishioners were wearing. Like all dogs, Ginny is very sensitive to new smells, and I could tell she was excited, although she behaved like a true lady. Her tail was going a mile a minute, her eyes were very bright in the light of the candles, and her black button nose was drinking in the rich mixture of aromas. Even to me, a mere human with a relatively insensitive nose, the church smelled exactly like Christmas.

But what seemed to excite Ginny the most were the smells and sight of all the strange animals—the hundreds of dogs and cats who were crowding into the church with their owners. There must have been at least five hundred of them, maybe more, because every seat in every pew was filled, both on the floor of the church and in the loft above, and more people were standing at the back, crowding in. Almost every one of them had brought at least one beloved pet.

Now you might think that in all that crowding you would hear the loud sounds of barking and hissing. You'd imagine a lot of tugging on leashes and growling as the dogs and cats checked one another out and looked with suspicious eyes at the strangers on all sides of them. Surprisingly, there wasn't. There was a lot of sniffing and some curious licking, but no fights broke out. I didn't hear even one canine or feline cuss word. It was as though the animals actually knew, through some mysterious instinct, that they were here to receive a blessing and that tonight was a very special time of the year, a holy time, the holiest.

Or maybe it was the soft organ music that was echoing through the church, a Bach prelude. Animals react very positively to music; when I was much younger I enjoyed reading Greek myths, and I learned that Orpheus could tame animals using only the sound of his musical instrument. The beasts would gather around him to listen, and even the most savage of them would not attack the smallest and most helpless while Orpheus was playing a song on his lyre. Tonight's organ music surely must have had a soothing effect on the hundreds of animals waiting in the church pews. Even the Chairman, who is a lively, squirmy, hyper little kitten, remained calm and peaceful in the arms of Ruth Jaffe. This was the first time I'd ever seen good-as-gold behavior from *that* little rascal.

Sitting next to us was Bill Edwards, community relations coordinator of the Barnes & Noble book chain. Bill is an animal lover and a big supporter of *The Dog Who Rescues Cats*. He himself has been rescuing cats for about five years and he's saved twenty of them, keeping twelve of them as his pets. Like me, he is especially interested in the rejects—the cats who have some handicap or disability that most people wouldn't accept in a pet. These pathetic creatures are his favorites, and under his care they blossom into wonderful pets.

Some weeks earlier, Bill had rescued a cat out of his

basement, an animal who was still wild and paranoid. She would not let Bill touch her. But that night, as Bill was getting ready to come to the church for the Blessing of the Animals, something wonderful happened. I'll let him tell the story in his own words.

BILL'S CHRISTMAS MIRACLE

"I've been feeding a colony of cats in my basement for a long time, but conditions became so bad down there that the cats were all infested with fleas and getting sick. So I trapped the cats and took them to the vet and had them cleaned up, inoculated, and neutered.

"One of them, a female kitten I named Cleopatra, I brought home to join my family, but she was so feral that I had to keep her locked in the bathroom so she wouldn't attack my other cats. I tried to get close to her, to stroke her and show her that she wasn't in any danger, but she didn't trust anybody. Cleo wouldn't let me touch her; she clawed me and bit me whenever I got too close. I was covered in scratches and teeth marks. Finally, I thought it was time to let Cleo have access to the rest of the apartment. The moment she was out of the bathroom she dashed under my bed and wouldn't leave, hiding there, refusing to come out even to eat. I wound up putting a food bowl and a litter pan under the bed, but that was an unsatisfactory arrangement.

"What I really wanted was to have Cleo join the family and be my pet, but I could see that I'd have to start from scratch (and I mean scratch!). It looked as though she'd have to go back to the bathroom, so I set up a small cat carrier there and put her food dish further and further back into it, with each meal luring her with food. I decided to try to bring her to church for the Blessing of the Animals. Maybe a Christmas miracle would happen, and Cleo would calm down and not be so frightened.

"On Christmas Eve, before going to the Blessing, I did a meditation. The subject of my meditation was the hope that Cleopatra would allow me to touch her. With Cleo in the carrier I took the subway from Brooklyn into Manhattan to the Central Presbyterian Church. On the train I took off my glove and tentatively opened Cleo's box. I put my bare hand in and touched her very lightly . . . and nothing happened. None of her usual wild and frantic scratching, no biting, no hissing. No distrust at all. Just an amazing peace and quiet and the feel of her fur under my fingers. For the first time, and during the entire trip, Cleopatra allowed me to stroke and pet her. And, once we were inside the church, the woman sitting next to me put her hand into the carrier and stroked Cleo, and Cleo appeared to enjoy it.

"That night, I was asleep in bed when I woke up to a weight pressing against me. It was Cleo, curled up against my body and purring her head off. From that night on, it was as though she'd always been with me, and had never once been wild. All her fears were forgotten, and I could stroke her whenever I wanted to. Cleo became my pet, sweet, gentle, loving, and . . . a pussycat."

"It was a gift from God," Bill told me, and he meant it. It was a statement I understood completely, because it has happened to me more than once that a wild cat had learned to trust and to love. It's always a gift from God.

As the owners and their pets settled down into the church pews, Ginny didn't stop wagging her tail or swiveling her head to look at everybody. She really wanted to join them, especially the cats; I could tell she was aching to groom a strange cat's fur, to touch noses with it and start up a game. Ginny is absolutely crazy about cats; she thinks that she's their mother. The more cats she can get into her household, the better she likes it.

My condo in Long Island has a strict rule: no more than ten cats to an apartment. Right now, between Sheilah and me we have nineteen cats housed in our two apartments, all of them rescued by Ginny, so we stay under the wire. If Ginny had her way, we would have at least one hundred cats and kittens for her to mother and play with. I think Ginny wanted to take home every cat and kitten in the church that night.

A wooden manger had been set up in front of the communion table. It was filled with Christmas greenery, ready to receive the Christ Child. The manger is symbolic of the animals of the field—the sheep, the cows, the donkeys—who kneeled down there to worship when Jesus was born.

The Reverend Pindar was wearing a full red robe, and over it a long stole, a scarf that trailed down the front of his garment. It was a special scarf, showing a large number of animals two by two, as they were when they entered Noah's Ark. There were a number of officers of the church—lay people with church duties—there to assist the pastor in the Blessing of the Animals, and they, too, were wearing identi-

The Blessing of the Animals service: Behind Ginny and me sits Phyllis Levy, holding the Chairman, who behaved like a gentleman.

cal stoles, although theirs were not the same length as the reverend's. Exactly how special these scarves were we would not learn until the end of the service.

There was an air of festivity around the church before the service began. The holiday itself is so joyous, and there were so many children and babies, cats, dogs, and other pets crowded into the pews. There's nothing like children and animals to liven things up. It was like one big block party. People were getting to know each other, patting one another's pets, asking their names and their pedigrees. Several folks came down the center aisle to where we were sitting to give Ginny a pat or a stroke and to say hello to her and me. I was surprised at the number of people who recognized us, since we hadn't yet been introduced by the Reverend Pindar. Maybe they'd seen one of our newspaper stories or read the article about Ginny in *Good Housekeeping*. Maybe they'd watched us on the "Sally Jessy Raphael" show, seen a segment about Ginny on a local news show, or heard us over the radio. At any rate, they seemed to be familiar with Ginny's amazing record of rescues, and they all wanted to give her a pat on the head and call her a "good girl." Ginny, of course, lapped up all their attention; she's a sponge as far as affection is concerned, and no amount of human praise can be too much for her. I wouldn't have believed that her tail could wag any harder, but it did.

WE ARE MADE WELCOME

It was now time to settle down. A hush fell over the pews, people went back to their seats, and all eyes turned to the communion table. The white-robed choir of young schoolgirls and schoolboys, the Children's Choir of the Central Presbyterian Church, was filing down the center aisle and taking their places in the carved wooden choir stall, singing. The choir led the congregation in that familiar Christmas hymn "O Come, All Ye Faithful," and the Reverend Pindar mounted the pulpit and raised his hands to begin. He started with a speech of welcome. "I want to extend a warm word of greeting to three communities with us here tonight," he began.

First, he welcomed all those who had come here for the first time. "Will you just raise a hand or a paw?" Everybody laughed, and many hands (and paws) shot into the air to let the others know who the first-timers were. "We welcome you tonight."

Secondly, the pastor welcomed the press, thanking them for their role in bringing the Central Presbyterian Church's Blessing of the Animals to the attention of so many people, helping it to grow from one year to the next into what he called "a New York evening." There were a number of media members present, reporters with tape recorders and television people with video cameras. There was even a special section roped off for them, with a sign saying "Media: Please Kneel or Sit Here," which I couldn't help smiling at. It's hard for me to picture busy reporters kneeling, but some of them did.

Then, of course, Reverend Pindar welcomed all the animals. "Last but not least, the creatures, God's creatures." As if it were a cue, a sudden chorus of barkings, yippings, yelpings, and meows filled the air, as though all the pets were saying, "Thank you, Reverend."

"I'm going to give you a chance to do what we've started doing over the last two or three years," the pastor went on. "Our pets have listened to us for a number of years, giving them welcome, barking commands, and hissing and meowing. But for tonight, just for tonight, think of the sound your animal makes." Then a sweet hush fell, and Reverend Pindar looked around at all of us.

"Listen to the sound of the silence," he told us quietly. "People tell me it's impossible to have four hundred fifty or five hundred people here with their animals, but hear the silence. I do believe that the Peaceable Kingdom must be like this. To waken us just a little, would you all *gently* make the sounds your animals make?"

A chorus of human barking, howling, and mewing, some of the imitations more convincing than others, rose up from the congregation, along with laughter. The real cats and dogs chimed in, and for a minute the church rocked with a loud and happy boisterous racket that bounced off the walls and echoed to the vaulted ceiling. I could only think of the line from the Old Testament, from the Psalms, "Make a joyful noise unto the Lord." This was surely one joyful noise. Ginny joined in happily, barking, and the little Chairman raised his kitten head and meowed in his silvery voice.

The pastor then extended a special welcome to two people, the first being Cleveland Amory, who is so well-known and well-loved for his wonderful books like *The Cat Who Came For Christmas* and *The Best Cat Ever*, both of them best-sellers, and for the wonderful unselfish work he has done with animals over so many years. When the pastor next called out my name, Philip Gonzalez, I felt a warm and happy glow of gratitude that Ginny's and my rescue work with homeless and abused cats was becoming so recognized, especially on such a special night as this. What an honor!

Reverend Pindar told us that a generous portion of the money collected in the Christmas Eve offerings would be donated to two special charities—to the Fund for Animals, its president and founder Cleveland Amory, and to POWARS, an organization that cares for the animals belonging to people in New York City who have AIDS and can't take care of their pets as well as they'd like to.

"Last but not least, welcome to all of you who return again and again," said the pastor, adding a fourth community to welcome. "For without the returnings, there wouldn't be many new beginnings."

We heard a reading from the Book of Isaiah, a beautiful foretelling of the birth of a redeemer, when the lion shall lie down with the sheep, and a little child shall lead them. It was read by Jeanne Baker, lector, while the choir responded with "O Come, O Come, Emmanuel," a moving hymn that is one of my own personal favorites.

The Reverend William H. Pindar read from the greatest story ever told, the birth of Jesus from the Book of St. Luke, about how the Holy Babe was born in a stable and laid in a manger. Then the pastor called Cleveland Amory, Phyllis Levy, Ginny, and myself up for the lighting of the Christ Candle. We moved up to the communion table. I was holding Ginny's leash tightly with my left hand because I don't have the full use of my right arm. The Christ Candle was the tallest one, the only one that had not been lit earlier. It symbolizes the birth of the Christ Child. Now that we had come to the part of the service when the birth of Jesus is accomplished, it was time for the unlit candle to take on life as well.

The Reverend Pindar praised my Ginny to the congregation, stating that she had rescued at least eleven cats and brought them all home. I don't know where he got that figure of eleven, because Ginny is responsible for almost twenty times that number! The congregation gasped out loud and broke into applause anyway. Imagine if they'd known how many cats Ginny had *really* saved from death! They might have carried her around the church on their shoulders.

The pastor held out a long taper that was burning brightly, and Cleveland, Phyllis, and I put our right hands on the taper next to the pastor's. Together, we lit the Christ Candle. My right hand wasn't strong enough to hold the taper alone, but surrounded by my friends' hands, it did its share. There was strength in our numbers. For me, this was a moment of great beauty and completion, like closing the magic circle of this holy evening. When we all exchanged a kiss of peace, I gave and received it gladly.

A tenor, George Garcia, who couldn't have been more than fourteen years old, raised his voice to tell us of a star whose light we all follow as it bends toward Bethlehem. When he finished his song, there was so much applause that all the dogs started barking.

Then Reverend Pindar took an infant into his arms with great pride and told us that it's not every time that a grandfather can read the Christmas story to his grandson for the first time. His little grandchild Keegan, only a few months old, cried all the way through the reading, which made everyone in the congregation smile and murmur "Aawww."

I truly enjoyed the pastor's sermon on Christmas Eve and the holy hilarity of it all.

"Holy hilarity reminds us that in what appears to be disorder and desperation and despair, there is something even deeper, more encouraging. It's a pattern that is called quite simply 'God is with us.' That is the holy part of the hilarity.

"Ginny, Ginny dear heart, you have gone out into the byways and highways, and have created holy hilarity," said the pastor. "This amazing dog has exercised compassion to degrees that I can't comprehend. She has brought home a blind cat. She has brought home a cat with no feet in the back to move. She has brought home a cat whose mind is a little gently turned so that the cat just rolls over, again and again and again."

My thoughts turned to the cats the pastor had mentioned—little blind Jackie, my dear Betty Boop who has no rear feet, sweet Topsy, so brain-damaged that she can't walk or even stand up. I felt tears of happiness stinging my eyelids because my angelic Ginny had saved them all from death, and they were now living safely and happily with Ginny and me. All damaged, yet all enjoying life. And Ginny was getting much deserved credit for it from the packed house of this beautiful church on Christmas Eve. I'm always proud of Ginny, but I've never been so proud of her in my life as I was right then.

The Reverend Pindar then told them of Ginny's other important rescue, when she saved my life. He actually read to the congregation from my book, *The Dog Who Rescues Cats*. He called it a spiritual message.

"'I am needed,'" he read, "'as I was never before needed in my life, by all the homeless and hungry mistreated animals. In my old life I had plenty of fun but no real happiness. . . . Little Ginny, part schnauzer, part Siberian husky, part angel from heaven, has taught me the most important lesson in life, that life is not worth living without love, that giving love is more rewarding than getting it, and that the humblest creatures, the least advantaged creatures, are worthy of the greatest outpouring of love. . . . If that's not heaven's message, I'd like to know what is.'"

Suddenly I felt proud of myself, too, for having been a part of Ginny's miraculous rescues, and for writing a book that was read aloud in church this Christmas Eve. I felt a glow of such satisfaction as I'd never quite felt before. It's one thing to be appreciated by my cats and my dog, but quite another thing to have strangers praising you.

As good as I felt with all of this attention, I was a little embarrassed by it, too, and I was glad when we began to sing "O, Little Town of Bethlehem," and the attention was off Ginny and me.

THE BLESSING OF THE ANIMALS

At last it was time for the great celebration, for the Blessing of the Animals. This was the reason all the pets had been brought here tonight. Without pushing, men, women, and children filed forward with their pet animals as we all sang "Silent Night" and the organ next played "What Child Is This?" It was as peaceful and happy as anything you have ever seen. A few at a time, they came up to the communion table where the pastor and his officers of the church stood in front of the manger ready to bless. People led their dogs on leashes or carried them in their arms; the cats rode high up on shoulders or looked down from the security of their owners' embraces.

Some of the pets were dolled up in bandannas or Santa Claus hats or fancy sweaters. One golden retriever was dressed in a fur coat, which startled me. Why would an animal wear the skin of another animal? It wouldn't, of course, if it had the choice, but its owner had made the choice for the dog. Another retriever was wearing white wings and a golden halo. His owner must think his dog is an angel. Why not? I know *mine* is. I saw pug dogs (one really fat pug was carried by a really fat man, and dog and owner looked exactly alike), spaniels, retrievers, a greyhound, beagles, Labradors, Yorkshire terriers and Jack Russells, Dalmatians, Samoyeds, West Highland and wire-haired terriers, Lhasa apsos, Shih Tzus, shar-peis, dachshunds, poodles, schnauzers, and some really fancy breeds I didn't even recognize. There were even a few mixed breeds, but not many. Pedigree or mixed breed, it didn't matter. Cats, dogs, frogs, hamsters, mice, turtles, guinea pigs, bowls of tropical fish, even a snake, all were greeted, blessed, stroked, and petted by the Reverend William H. Pindar and his lay officers of the church. I couldn't get over how much like the Peaceable Kingdom this was. With all the activity, there was no fighting and no biting, just quiet love from the humans and a surprising amount of patience on the part of the animals.

Ginny was tugging eagerly at her leash as the animals were paraded by her from the back of the church. I could tell from her furiously wagging tail and the brightness in her eyes that she wanted to kiss and groom all the cats and take a good sniff at all the dogs. In all my life I never saw a friendlier animal than Ginny; she's in love with just about everything that lives.

Flashbulbs kept going off as proud owners took snapshots of their pets receiving their blessings. There were videotape cameras, too. I'd brought my own camera, but in the excitement of the evening I forgot to use it.

A couple of people even brought stuffed animals—toys, like teddy bears. Perhaps these people (and not all of them were children) had lost a pet or the pet was ill at home; maybe they only had stuffed toys to love. The teddy bears and one stuffed Opus the penguin were blessed as solemnly as the live animals. One woman I'll never forget. She brought a box in which was a beloved little Yorkie, together with her litter of puppies! Each cute little pup was dressed in a warm sweater and each was lifted out of the box in turn and received its own blessing and a kiss on its tiny head.

When every animal had been blessed, including Ginny and the Chairman, the Reverend Pindar and his officers of the church remained lined up side by side, facing the congregation. He called everyone's attention to the long stoles they were wearing, pointing out that they depicted the animals saved from destruction by Noah's Ark. Then the pastor reminded us that, at the end of the Flood, Noah had sent another creature, a dove, to locate dry land. The dove had returned with an olive branch in its beak as proof of life still existing on earth, after which God set a rainbow in the heavens as His covenant of peace with humankind. Then, turning over the stoles, the pastor and his officers of the church showed us that the undersides of the scarves were woven into a rainbow. They all stretched out their smaller rainbows to make one big one, and they wished us peace. It was a beautiful end to a beautiful evening, and we were all very moved.

The service was over, we sang "Joy to the World," kisses of peace were exchanged by all, and people began to file out of the church. The Reverend Pindar approached Ginny and me, asking us if we would mind remaining behind to stay for the second service. For the first time since the Central Presbyterian Church had instituted the Blessing of the Animals, they were holding two services in the same evening, the second one to accommodate all the people and animals who were waiting outside because there'd been no more room in the church. Of course we agreed. We were happy that this wonderful evening would not yet come to an end.

Riding in the car back to Long Island after the second service, Sheilah and I were subdued and spoke very little. I know that she was still feeling the effects of our wonderful experience. My mind was filled with the sights and the sounds of tonight's Blessing of the Animals, and with the holy solemnity of Christmas Eve. Ginny was curled up by my side, while the Chairman was sound asleep in my lap, rolled into a little ball with his paws over his eyes. In my

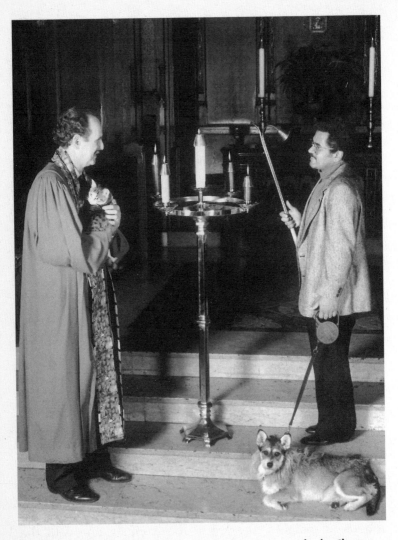

The Blessing of the Animals service: At the later service, I lit the Christ Candle by myself, while the Reverend Pindar gave the Chairman a Christmas cuddle.

memory I was still experiencing the glowing fullness of the celebration—the sweet-smelling candles, the colorful poinsettias, the powerful singing of the hymns, the happy gospel, the readings from Isaiah and Luke, the sermon, and especially the outpouring of love and peace on all the people and animals in the church. This had been one of the most beautiful evenings of my life; I felt privileged to be a part of it and honored to have had the Reverend Pindar read out loud from my book to the congregation. The emotions I was experiencing were almost overwhelming.

But I was starting to come down off this high. Mingled with the pride and happiness of this special occasion, I felt a deep sadness. The animals who had gathered in the Central Presbyterian Church this evening had all been beloved pets, even pampered pets, to judge by the looks of them. I remembered the dog in the fur coat. After all, the parishioners lived in one of the wealthiest neighborhoods of New York City, and the church itself was on ritzy Park Avenue. The great majority of the dogs I saw in church that night were fancy breeds; probably most of them came from good kennels and had pedigrees a yard long and papers of registry. I don't think I saw more than a dozen mixed-breed animal shelter pups like Ginny being walked or carried down the aisles. A large number of the cats were exotic breeds like Persians and Himalayans and Siamese. These animals lived charmed lives and enjoyed many blessings already—loving homes, food in their bellies, the best of care, warm places to sleep, and, most of all, the chance to give and receive devotion on a daily basis. They had their own people who always interacted with them in the most loving way. They enjoyed pats and cuddles, pet names, toys and games, special treats, warm laps, affectionate human hands raised only to stroke them, human lips and arms to give them kisses and hugs. For these pets, the Christmas Eve Blessing of the Animals was something extra, like the cherry on top of the whipped cream on top of the cake.

I thought about my indoor cats waiting for me at home. All of them had once been abandoned and homeless, some were disabled, most of them had been abused, and they'd had more than their share of misery, but now they'd come home. At last there was a protective roof over their heads, and they were warm and fed. Most of all, they were loved, and had become cherished and important members of Ginny's and my family.

I thought also about my outdoor cats, the eighty or so homeless street cats we feed twice a day; at least their bellies are full and we get them medical attention when it's needed. We find homes for them whenever we can. For street cats, their lives aren't as sad as most because Ginny, Sheilah, and I look after them daily.

But what about that vast, miserable army of homeless dogs and cats who wander freezing, starving, and diseased through our alleys and streets? Who is there to bless them? For these poor animals there is truly no room at the inn. Their lives are short and wretched, and they suffer greatly. Yet, if animals have souls—which I firmly believe they do— these unwanted creatures deserve a blessing as much as that coddled little Yorkie with the ribbon in its topknot or the Siamese cat in the fancy green leather harness who had been granted God's blessing in the church tonight.

If only every cat and dog in the world could have a home with an affectionate human who takes it to be blessed by God on Christmas Eve, and who blesses it with his or her own love on the other 364 days of the year! Too often humans can be cruel instead of kind, and people heartlessly abandon animals to fend for themselves and die. They don't have their animals neutered, then they throw the unwanted kittens away like garbage. These are hard realities to face, but Ginny and I face them daily in our rescue work.

Tears came into my eyes and I have to tell you I wasn't ashamed of them.

It was late, and Ginny, Sheilah, and I were all exhausted and feeling drained. We all knew that as soon as we reached home we would go right back out again to feed the street cats. I'd take off my best clothes and get into my jeans and my boots. Then we'd load up Sheilah's Camry with canned and dry cat food, fresh water, clean dishes, and off we'd drive to the eight feeding stations where the eighty home-less cats on our route were probably already waiting anx-iously for their supper, mewing and pacing the icy sidewalks. It was Christmas Eve for them, too, and this nutritious evening meal would be our own special Blessing of the Animals.

Ginny and the Chairman; it's sometimes hard to tell who belongs to whom.

Chapter 2

The Chairman

*F*IRST, I'D LIKE TO FILL YOU IN on some of the things that have happened to me since I wrote *The Dog Who Rescues Cats.* If you read that book, you know that my dog Ginny is in the lifesaving business, and that the first life she ever saved was mine. Ginny is a bright-eyed, tail-wagging, medium-sized mixed breed—mostly schnauzer and Siberian husky by the look of her—who came to me out of a Long Island animal shelter on one of the darkest days of my life.

I was a well-paid construction worker, content with my comfortable life, when an industrial accident cost me the use of my right arm. After my surgery all I could do was feel sorry for myself until my good friend Sheilah Harris convinced me to adopt a dog from our local shelter. She knew I needed some responsibility to snap me out of my depression. I agreed to adopt a large, male dog of a pure breed, but once I was in the animal shelter some instant mysterious connection that I can't explain took place between me and a smallish dog of no pedigree at all. The next thing I knew, I was head over heels in love with a pup I named Ginny. I took her home with me and we've been together ever since, six happy years.

Very soon she became the bright spot in an otherwise dark life. The more I came to know her, the brighter my life became, until Ginny and I were walking side by side in the light. She made all the difference to me between despair and fulfillment.

When I took Ginny home, I had no idea of how radically my life would change in such a short time. It turned out that Ginny Gonzalez was put on earth to save the lives of abandoned and homeless cats, especially disabled cats and kittens. With her it was a sacred mission. Using a kind of sixth sense, she would seek them out in the hardest-to-reach places, where I was certain that nothing could possibly survive. Ginny proved me wrong again and again, until I learned to trust her instincts completely. Time after time, she would turn up some ill, injured, disabled, abused, helpless cat or kitten and demand quick assistance for them. The more a cat needed her help, the faster Ginny was to respond.

Little by little, and at first with great reluctance on my part, Ginny increased my household from two—Ginny and me—to many more, all of the new ones being cats she rescued. When she started out, I was pretty much indifferent to cats. I really preferred dogs, but it wasn't long before

Ginny convinced me to love them as much as she does. We have a deaf cat, a cat with one eye, a cat with no hind feet, a cat so brain-damaged it can't stand up or walk, but rolls across the floor instead. We have a half-blind cat who was completely blind when we got her. Thanks to surgery she now can see out of one eye. The more a cat was disabled or abused, the more determined Ginny was to bring that animal straight home to her house, where she could look after it properly.

Apart from what she did for the cats, what Ginny did for me was also nothing short of a miracle. She found a depressed, disabled man and turned him into a useful, happy, functioning human being. And she did it all by her angelic example, through her kindness and her affection and her determination to make life better for others.

Almost as miraculous was the conversion of my friend and neighbor Sheilah, who was responsible for my adopting Ginny in the first place. Although she is kindness personified and a great dog lover, Sheilah had always felt a deep loathing for cats. Watching her beloved Ginny perform her amazing rescues, Sheilah learned not to fear the little creatures. Instead, she came to regard them with deep sympathy and affection. Today, her home is overflowing with cats and love, just as mine is, and she's known around the neighborhood as "the Cat Lady."

In addition to my indoor cats, I have about eighty or more outdoor cats, homeless strays whom Ginny, Sheilah, and I feed twice a day every day no matter the weather. Since the first book came out, we've expanded our feeding stations to eight and doubled the number of the cats we feed, so it takes a lot more time and patience and a lot more food and water. The trunk of Sheilah's Camry (she's no longer driving the Chevy Nova) is fitted out to carry as much food and water as we need.

We go wherever the cats are; homeless cats tend to congregate into communities, but the groups also tend to move around, looking for better shelter or more often because humans chase them away. Wherever they go, we find them and set up a new feeding station where they are already gathering. We check them out every day to make sure they're in good shape; if they need medical attention, we rush them to our veterinarian at the All Creatures Veterinary Clinic for treatment. We try to catch each and every one of them for neutering so they won't breed any more homeless animals, and we always try to find the right family for them. As of today, when I write this, thanks to Ginny's rescue efforts and the cooperation of Dr. Lewis Gelfand, DVM, our wonderful veterinarian, we've had the good luck to get close to eighty street cats into good and loving homes.

There's a kind of special squadron of outdoor cats; these are independent street cats who are willing to spend their nights in shelters I provide on my terrace, but who are off like a shot the next day when the sun comes up. They prefer the freedom of the streets to the confines of even the most loving home. I have put a string of cat carriers out on my terrace, lined with old blankets and warm towels, and a few regulars jump up there to spend their nights in some comfort, as though staying in a motel. But these cats enjoy checking out of the "motel" every day, not wanting to trade their free outdoor life for the chance to become pampered pets.

Among those "motel" cats was one I was very fond of, a white tom with a tiger-striped back, a white belly, and striped patches on its face who had a confident swagger that reminded me of Frank Sinatra. I called him the Chairman, because Sinatra is nicknamed "the Chairman of the Board." When he disappeared in the summer of 1995 it just about broke my heart. One day the Chairman was there, eating well and sleeping on my terrace, the next day he wasn't. I looked for him everywhere, twice a day, wherever I saw or fed our street cats. Once or twice I thought I saw him, but it always turned out to be a different cat with similar markings. It was never the Chairman. To this day, I still haven't given up hope. I know that street cats' lives are often too short and always too dangerous, and that the chances are good he was hit by a car or met up with a vicious dog, but I don't like to think about those chances. To me, the Chairman is still alive out there somewhere, swaggering around and enjoying life.

GINNY BECOMES FAMOUS

After the book came out, Ginny became something of a celebrity, especially in the small town in which I live. Wherever we go, we're recognized, or, to tell the truth, *Ginny* is recognized. Some people saw us on television after we appeared on the "Sally Jessy Raphael" show, New York City news shows, and CNN, while others had read Ginny's story in *Newsday*, our Long Island newspaper. Still others had actually read the book, either because they bought it or because they took it out of the library. Many of the kids had enjoyed visits from Ginny and me in their schoolrooms, and they are especially delighted to bump into her on our walks. "Ginny!" they yell as soon as they see her, and her tail goes crazy with happy wagging.

As we walked down the street, we soon got used to hearing, "Hey mister, is that the dog who saves cats? Is that the dog I saw on television?" Everybody wanted to pat Ginny on the head and ask me questions about her. They regard her as a hero. Recently, while we were out together on a stroll, a man stopped the taxi he was riding in to tell us what good work we were doing.

Ginny loves all the attention, but it doesn't turn her head. She knows she has a job to do—to continue to sniff out cats who need help and come to their aid—and she hasn't slowed down yet. On the contrary, she keeps on with her rescues and still shows us that unexplainable, uncanny ability to find injured or distressed cats where nobody else would think to look.

TYPICALLY GINNY GONZALEZ

Not long ago, we were feeding at one of our stations, a location near a gas station with a yard full of junked and abandoned vehicles. We always feed the cats underneath a large truck because the strays seem more comfortable staying crouched under something than venturing out into the open. Also, it's warmer there. I have a special stick that I use to push the food bowls under the vehicles and pull them out again when they're empty.

There was a pickup truck parked nearby that belonged to a landscaping company; its open truck bed was filled with sod and heavy grass clippings. The cab was empty; the driver was probably at lunch. Ginny ran to it, jumped right up into the truck, and began digging through the packed sod, concentrating on the area right under a heavy rake.

I came running after her to get her to stop, but by the time I reached her, she had already dug down to where a small cat was pinned under the rake, unable to move. Somebody— probably the truck driver—had piled many pounds of grass clippings on top of her, I guess because he never saw her. Under Ginny's anxious supervision I set the cat free. She was very close to being smothered, and she mewed pitifully as I brushed the grass and sod off her. I was holding a little beauty, a black-and-white adolescent no more than four months old with big, bright eyes and a happy expression. As soon as she was out of danger, she began to purr at the top of her lungs.

I took her home, and I named her Ms. Hunt, after a teacher in one of the classrooms that Ginny and I visit. The following day, I brought Ms. Hunt to Dr. Gelfand's office for her shots. I asked if he could place her with a loving owner. That very same afternoon, a man phoned my veterinarian and asked specifically, "Do you happen to have a cat for adoption that Ginny the dog rescued? I read the book, and I want to help Ginny out."

Dr. Gelfand mentioned Ms. Hunt, Ginny's latest kitten salvage, and a couple of days later the man showed up. One look, and the man and the cat fell in love. In less time than it takes to tell, that purring little bundle of charm was on her way to her new home with her new friend and protector.

Not long after that, Ginny, Sheilah, and I were out on our nighttime round of feeding when Ginny dashed away from us and ran toward a fence that had barbed wire on top of it. She began to whimper, a sure sign that a cat was in trouble and needed help. When we got to the fence we saw to our horror that a terrified cat was caught on the barbed wire, hanging there, unable to get down. She was struggling desperately, which only made her situation worse. The barbed wire was really cutting into her.

This was a problem, because I have only my left hand to work with, and a frightened cat needs two good hands. But Ginny put her paws up on the fence and whimpered straight at the cat, as though talking to her, and the cat heard her, stopped its struggling, braced itself, gave a sudden leap, and tore itself free, landing at our feet.

If there was ever a situation in which a cat would run for its life and hide itself somewhere to lick its wounds, this was it. But this cat didn't run away. Instead, it went straight up to Ginny and rubbed against her affectionately, as though saying "thanks for finding me." Next it went to Sheilah and did the same thing. It avoided me. We recognized that cat as one we'd been feeding for a while, so I put the hood up on my jacket, just as I always wear it up when we are putting the food down. When I looked as I always do when feeding, the cat recognized me, too, and said its thanks.

I realized then that all the rescues that I'd helped Ginny make have given me a real insight into cats' thinking; a few years ago it would never have occurred to me to put my hood up in order to set a terrified cat's mind at ease.

We took the cat home with us and checked its wounds from the barbed wire. Large clumps of its fur were torn out, but there were only a few cuts in its flesh, none of them deep enough to have damaged a vital organ. We dressed those. The cat turned out to be female, around six months old, with a really sweet face and a beautiful, friendly nature. I named her Roosevelt. She found a home right away, and it was a special home. Sheilah's own mother and father took her in and gave her a very pretty new name, Minouche, which is French for "little one."

I think of these rescues as typically Ginny Gonzalez. In both cases, neither Sheilah nor I saw or heard anything out of the ordinary. It took Ginny's own personal radar to detect the trouble from a distance. If she hadn't dug so frantically for Ms. Hunt, the kitten would almost certainly have died of suffocation under all that grass and sod. If she hadn't led us straight to Roosevelt, it's very likely that the cat would have injured herself much more severely while struggling on the barbed wire. The trapped cats were no doubt mewing their heads off, but the frantic sounds didn't carry to human ears from far away. Humans don't possess the keen senses that dogs do, especially Ginny, who has instincts in spades. I'm not sure that any other dog, no matter how keen its hearing, would have detected and responded to those cries for help as Ginny did.

Ginny's instincts alone saved Ms. Hunt and Roosevelt. As usual, her special "radar of the heart" led her straight to those helpless cats in danger, and Sheilah and I just tagged along to do the mopping up.

WHITE TIE AND TAILS

We were feeding cats one night at the gas station where there are so many abandoned cars and junked trucks, the same place we found little Ms. Hunt. Suddenly, Ginny ran over to a wrecked car and began to whimper that special sound she makes to let me know a cat is in trouble. I know that sound by heart, and Ginny is never wrong. I figured some cat must be hiding under there, maybe hurt or even disabled, so I got a flashlight and went to have a look.

There was a cat under the car all right, stretched out stiff as a board. I took hold of the stick I use to retrieve my empty cat bowls and prodded it gently; I was afraid to touch it in case I picked up some disease that might infect my housecats and outdoor cats. She was dead, no doubt about it. Rigor mortis had already set in. But Ginny wouldn't stop her whimpering; if anything, she whimpered even louder. She raised one front foot for emphasis, pawing at the car.

"See, Ginny, the poor thing is dead. There's nothing I can do," I told her. "I'll take her over to the shelter and they'll bury her."

But what I told her made no impression on Ginny, who continued to whimper and scratch at the car. I know Ginny pretty well by now, and she doesn't make those sounds just to hear her own voice. I switched the flashlight on again and peered under the vehicle once more. At first, I saw nothing.

Suddenly, a tiny head popped up, and then another.

There were two baby kittens hiding underneath that car, a pair of tuxedos, little black-and-whites. With Ginny guarding them anxiously, I pulled them out very gently and took a look at them.

They were so small that both of them fit into my hand at the same time. They were somewhere between ten days and two weeks old, and their eyes were barely open. The pair of them kept giving out high-pitched little squeaks of hunger and fear. Every time they squealed, Ginny's ears pricked in reply. She had stopped her whimpering because she knew that I was now on the case.

I could picture what must have happened. The poor dead cat Ginny had found must be their mother. Maybe she'd been poisoned, maybe she'd been hit by a car. But, even in pain, even dying, she had dragged herself back to her kittens. Cats are very good mothers, protective of their babies and anxious when their kittens are out of sight.

Those kittens were a banner rescue for Ginny and me, and we took them home right away to clean them up and begin restoring the breath of life with nourishing food. I gave them warm goat's milk from a special feeding bottle, plus a special kitten formula, KMR, that I get from the veterinarian. The bottles and the formula are supplies I always have on hand; they've come in handy many more times than once. The kittens ate every hour on the hour, their scrawny little bellies growing round and plump. When they weren't eating, they were sleeping, curled up tightly against Ginny's warm belly. They purred in their sleep. My wonderful dog lay quietly beside them without moving, except to wash them from time to time with her maternal tongue, reassuring them that they were now safe.

The following day, I carried them both to the vet. Although at first I feared for their lives because they were so young, there was nothing wrong with those kittens except starvation. Once they were out of danger and you couldn't see their ribs, they were as cute as kittens get, playing with Ginny's tail, tumbling over each other, and batting at imaginary butterflies. They were perfect little subjects for adoption, an adorable pair of brothers, and I named them Black and White.

The kittens were about four weeks old in October, when the St. Francis of Assisi holy day is celebrated in my local Catholic church by a Blessing of the Animals. I took them to be blessed by the priest, and also to find homes for them. Who could be better for us to ask than people coming to that service? They must already be feeling affection for animals, so I knew that Black and White would get loving owners.

Sheilah and I went from person to person after the mass, asking, "Would you like to adopt a kitten?" We held them up and they were so appealing I didn't think anybody could resist them. But you'd be surprised how many people can say no, even in the face of all that cuteness. At last, a woman with a Dalmatian dog took one of the kittens, Black, because the dog and the cat matched, both with black-and-white fur.

As to the fate of White, about a week later Sheilah took him to a Pet Expo in Rockville Centre, where one of the vendors snapped him up and promised a loving home. Ginny's score for cat rescues went up by two more.

THE CHAIRMAN COMES BACK

Ginny's next rescue, about a week after White was adopted, was one of the most dramatic of her career, almost equal to her miraculous discovery of that litter of five new-born kittens abandoned in a large sewer pipe at a construction site. I still don't understand how she found them. I didn't hear a single mew, but she saved five lives that day. All of them survived, did well, and found good homes, mostly with me and with Sheilah.

I told you that the Chairman disappeared in August of 1995 and hasn't been spotted since. Well, across the street from the animal shelter is a glassworks where windows are manufactured, the Airtite Window factory. Because there's a lot of broken glass around, I don't let Ginny go onto the factory's loading dock, but we do have a feeding station very close by, just across the street. For her safety, I keep Ginny in the car when we feed there. I just tell her "stay." Usually she stays put, because Ginny is always very responsive to what I say to her, but this time she dashed out of the car and ran to my side.

First, she froze and stood at attention, staring at the loading dock. Her nose twitched and her ears stood up as stiffly as palace guards. It doesn't take a genius to know when a dog is sensing something, but I could tell she was even more excited than usual. Suddenly, before I could make a move to stop her, Ginny was heading across the street at a dead run, straight for the loading platform. Before we knew what was happening, Ginny ran down the ramp and began digging furiously in a carton overflowing with broken glass.

I gasped in horror. Broken glass!

"Ginny! No!" I yelled, and Sheilah let out a scream. We both ran toward the loading dock to stop her. I could tell my dog was cutting her pads on the sharp glass, maybe deeply, but Ginny paid us no attention. She kept on pawing through the knifelike shards with all her energy. Nothing could stop her. By the time we reached the platform, she had found something, picked it up in her mouth, and was already limping toward us with the something dangling from her jaws. Although it was dark out, there was a light on the loading dock, and I could see that Ginny was leaving bloody footprints. My heart sank. How badly was she hurt?

As to what was in her mouth, it was a curled-up ball of fur, barely moving. At first I thought it was a baby raccoon. That made me uneasy, because the mother might be very close by and raccoons don't take kindly to their babies being mouth-carried by a strange dog. Also, there's a scare in the Northeast about raccoons with rabies. Many of them do carry that dread disease. I kind of like raccoons, because I have respect for every creature on earth, but I'm careful to keep my distance from them. And here was my dog with one in her mouth!

"Ginny, put that down!" I ordered, but she just kept coming, trotting forward until she reached Sheilah and me. Ginny didn't seem to notice that her paws were bleeding as she laid the little bundle down at our feet.

Suddenly, it uttered a tiny little sound, an unmistakable mew. I sighed in relief. It was a kitten, very tiny, and it was

covered with splinters of glass. Some of the glass had pene-
trated its skin, and its fur was bloody. It was a sight that
would make a marble statue shed tears. Who could do such
a cruel thing to one of God's helpless creatures? Could this
kitten possibly live?

But even this injured kitten was not our first priority. We
wanted to get Ginny home right away so we could examine
her wounds and treat them. Sheilah scooped her up and carried her to the car in her arms, even though Ginny is no
lightweight. I followed with the kitten.

As soon as we were safe in my apartment, Sheilah and I
brought Ginny into the bathroom and turned on the light
for a good look. My dog sat quietly, letting us examine her
without pulling her paws out of our hands, even though they
must have been hurting.

There were pieces of glass stuck in the pads of Ginny's
feet. We lifted them out very carefully, making sure to get
even the tiniest piece out, washed her wounds, and applied
a styptic pencil, the same pencil I use when I cut myself
shaving. We then turned our attention to the kitten, which
couldn't have been more than a week and a half old. Gently,
we brushed the glass off it, pulling out the pieces sticking in
its flesh, and examined its scratches and cuts. They didn't
appear to be too serious, so we went the soap-and-water-
and-styptic-pencil route with the little cat, too. Tomorrow
morning I would examine the wounds of our two adventur-
ers and see if they needed stitching up and veterinary attention.

Meanwhile, the little cat was desperate for food, so we
got out the little bottle we use for nursing kittens and gave

the baby a decent meal, goat's milk and KMR. The kitten drank until it was full, and then curled up and went to sleep between Ginny's aching paws. It was already making itself at home.

To tell you the truth, neither Sheilah nor I expected that baby kitten to live. Its wounds weren't serious (and neither were Ginny's), but it just seemed to be too young to have much of a chance at growing up. There was a feistiness in that little fellow, though, and it surprised us by thriving. A few days later it was as lively as a kitten ought to be, and eating enough for six. I noticed something then for the first time. The markings on the baby's coat of fur were almost identical to the Chairman's, a white body with patches of tiger-striping. It was a male, too, like the Chairman. And, like the Chairman, this kitten had "attitude." He was exactly like my lost outdoor cat in miniature—feisty, independent, and very intelligent.

I felt in my heart that God had sent this kitten to me because I was still missing the Chairman so much. I made up my mind there and then not to put him up for adoption, but to keep him. It would be a double reward: a reward to Ginny, because she had gone through so much to rescue this baby and didn't want to give him up, and a reward to me, for helping Ginny with her work. I'd get my cat back again, and this time he'd be an indoor cat with no risk of running away or getting hit by a car.

I named him the Chairman, and it was this little cat who was lying so peacefully in Ruth Jaffe's arms the night of the Blessing of the Animals. The Chairman and Ginny have a very special relationship of affection; she seems to think he belongs to her, the way she fusses over him all the time. And he thinks he belongs to her, too. It's almost as though the Chairman recognizes that he's Ginny's living reward for her bravery in diving into that box of broken glass. So he's God's gift to both of us.

The Chairman was a quick study, that little guy, and he caught on to cat food very early. Weaning him off the bottle was no trouble at all; the first time he sniffed the canned food, his tiny face went down into that dish and didn't come up for air until the bowl was empty. As soon as we moved the Chairman to Sheilah's apartment, he began to miss Ginny. When my dog made her daily visits to the Harris cats, he would desert them all and run over to Ginny for a cuddle and a tongue-bath. In fact, when Ginny wasn't around the Chairman seemed to become depressed, not his usual happy self, and he would actually cry. So first we brought Ginny down more often, and later we gave up and moved the kitten back to my apartment for several hours every day, so he could be with his "mommy."

That kitten is quite a ham, and he's become a media star. He's done quite a number of talk shows, and has been to school with me and Ginny to show the children a life that was saved. These days, whenever Ginny appears in print or on TV, she's usually photographed with the Chairman. The broken-glass rescue has captured everybody's imagination; *Newsday* did a feature on it, and so did *The National Enquirer*. All any photographer has to do is aim a camera at the Chairman and the kitten takes a great pose, just like a model. The rescue of the Chairman has come to symbolize Ginny's special gifts and her bravery; the two of them are a

Ginny in doggie bliss, with the Chairman (left) and Caesar (right) grooming her.

pair now, inseparable, and nothing will ever break them up.

I still miss the original Chairman, and I still think he'll turn up some day, that one night he'll jump up on my terrace and take his place among my outdoor cats again. I haven't given up hope. When he does come back, I'll give the little one a new name, Chairman Too.

A catnapper and a dognapper catching a snooze.

CHAPTER 3

GINNY LEARNS HER ABCS

*A*NYBODY WHO'S READ MY FIRST BOOK, *The Dog Who Rescues Cats,* has already met most of the cats in my household and Sheilah's, and is aware of how Ginny found them in strange, hidden places, saved them, and brought them home. But a few names will be new and strange even to my old readers—Blondie, Clippie, King Arthur, Vinola— because these are cats we've adopted since the first book was written, and I think this might be the place to tell their stories briefly.

BLONDIE

Blondie is a pale brown cat who looks blond in dim light. She was one of the outside cats we feed every day; her feeding station was by the tree. Whenever we got there with the food, Blondie would push herself forward until she was right up close to Ginny, then she'd start a game with her and the two of them would play together. Lulu was another cat in the group; when I noticed that she had a small injury on her back, possibly from a run-in with another cat, I knew she had to go to the vet. So the next time I came with food I brought a cat carrier with me. When Blondie saw the carrier, she jumped into it and wouldn't come out.

"Okay," I told her, "I guess I was wrong. It must be your turn and not Lulu's." It was a great opportunity to get Blondie spayed and inoculated, and I wasn't going to pass it up. So we brought her to Dr. Gelfand's office. When he examined her and tested her blood, he broke the news to us: Blondie was FIV-positive; she had feline AIDS.

"Should I put her to sleep?" the vet asked. "It's probably the kindest thing."

"No way! She's Ginny's friend, and Ginny would never forgive either one of us. Treat her."

Blondie stayed at the vet's for four months, not getting any better, but not getting any worse, either. Sadly, there's not a whole lot a vet can do with a cat who has AIDS. What she really needed was a home, and love. Ginny was more than ready to supply both, so we brought Blondie home, FIV and all. I keep her under supervision, so that she doesn't get into any fights with my other cats, because we can't afford any blood contamination. Most of the time she lives in a very large cage, separated from the rest of the cats outside in the room, yet a part of everything that's going on. From time to time, when I'm home with all of them, I let her out for a while to mingle. She has a home with Ginny and me as long as she lives.

CLIPPIE

Clippie is a female orange and white tiger kitten who was sitting alone in a cage in my local animal shelter. Ginny, Sheilah, and I often visit the shelter where I found Ginny because Ginny is very fond of the animals in the cages. She's especially fond of Kenny Colon, who cared for her in Ginny's own shelter days after she was brought there close to death from neglect and starvation. It was Ken who talked me into taking Ginny out for that very first walk the day she and I met, when I insisted I didn't want the little female dog, but a large one, preferably a male. I had my eye on a Doberman pinscher, but Kenny was persistent. He didn't give up shoving the little dog at me until I agreed to walk her around the block. And you know what happened. We came back from that walk firmly bonded to each other. So both of us owe Kenny a lot. We always bring the cats in the cages the munchies they love to snack on.

Ginny ran right up to Clippie's cage and began making that "Gimme, gimme, gimme" whimper I know so well. It always means "I want that cat. I have to have that cat."

"Absolutely not, Ginny!" I told her. "We've got enough cats." If I believe Ginny is ever going to pay attention to me on that subject I need to have my head examined.

The fact that she was in a cage all by herself aroused my curiosity. I asked about the marmalade kitten, and why she was alone. Ken told us this puss's sad story. As pretty as she is, she was adopted not once but twice. Both owners brought her back to the shelter, complaining that she was too paranoid and unfriendly. As a feral cat, she could not easily make the big adjustment to get along with people, but would hide under the furniture and not let anybody come near her. Neither of her adopted families had the patience to let the little marmalade take her own time to calm down, learn to trust, and make friends. Now she was considered unadoptable. And there's only one end for an unadoptable kitty.

"That cat's gonna be put down tomorrow," Kenny said sadly.

When I heard that I could feel tears stinging my eyelids. I glanced at Ginny, and she was looking at me with the most reproachful, imploring look in her large brown eyes.

How did Ginny know? She must have read my thoughts. She really wanted to save that young cat's life. I couldn't stand the look any more than I could stand the idea of that pretty, healthy little cat being put to sleep. And then, like the icing on the cake, Ginny began that old familiar whimper that tells me, "I've got to have that cat!"

So she joined our family, and I named her Clippie after the nickname that Cleveland Amory's brother gave him, and because she had been rescued from the jaws of death which were already clip-clip-clipping at her.

The first night that Clippie stayed with us she came right

up on the bed and slept with me, Ginny, and the other cats. She kept licking my face. So much for her paranoia and hostility. It was Ginny who made the big difference; with Ginny Clippie felt safe for the first time in her life. All she needed to become peaceable was to be shown that she was welcome and loved, and Ginny did that by grooming her and staying very close to her, cuddling her while she was eating, and guarding her when the other cats sniffed around the kitten a little too aggressively or growled at her.

Clippie is a loving, lovable pet and a great friend of Ginny's. It seems as though she recognizes Ginny as her savior from her death sentence. I'm her second-string savior, I guess, because she follows Ginny and me all around my apartment. This was another one of Ginny's rescues; she discovered that cat in her cage in the same way that she discovered the Chairman under the broken glass, by the use of her special lifesaving radar. Otherwise, why did she run straight up to that cage of all cages and select that cat of all cats, the one doomed to be put to sleep the next day? Why did she keep giving me that "Gimme . . . gimme that cat" whimper that she knows darn well I can never resist? That special sixth sense of hers, which I call Ginny's radar of the heart, was certainly working overtime that day.

KING ARTHUR

King Arthur's story is very different. He was one of the outdoor cats whom we feed at the Market Street feeding station. He was a bully, pushing everybody around except Ginny.

When she first encountered him, Ginny went down on her belly and crawled toward him in the same way that she crawls toward small children; it means, "You have no reason to be afraid of me." Ginny uses the crawl very judiciously, and only to a few cats. She seems to understand instinctively when and how it will work to calm a frightened or aggressive cat. King Arthur responded by becoming her friend on the spot. Whenever we turned up with the food, King Arthur would shove the other cats out of his way until he was the one standing closest to Ginny. He demanded all of her attention, and was very jealous of any of the other cats getting close to my dog, whom he obviously thought of as *his* dog. King Arthur would also make the first lunge for the food, so that the other cats at the feeding site would run away and hide.

His aggressiveness was a problem for me and for the other homeless cats, and I set out to solve it. One day I scooped King Arthur up in the carrier and took him to the veterinarian, thinking that if he were neutered he might become less bullying and aggressive. To my great surprise, Dr. Gelfand told me that King Arthur was not only already neutered, he was also declawed! Obviously, he had been somebody's pet housecat and had lost his home. Had he run away? Gotten lost? Or had some unfeeling person just dumped him out in the street to fend for himself without claws? I'll never know. All I know for sure is that he was deprived of his home. No wonder he was aggressive! It's an even greater wonder he'd survived at all.

I felt so sorry for King Arthur I was tempted to take him home myself, but I already had just about all the cats I could manage. So I put notices up for him, offering King Arthur to a good home. We actually did find a family for him, but the new owners brought him back to Dr. Gelfand's office because King Arthur wouldn't use the litter box.

So, once again, he was a cat without a home. I guarantee I would not have adopted him if it weren't for Ginny. I was getting ready to leave the All Creatures Veterinary Clinic, leaving King Arthur behind with Dr. Gelfand, and I tugged on her leash, but Ginny refused to come. She wouldn't budge. Instead, she sat firmly by King Arthur's side, making it very plain that she was determined not to leave without him. And Ginny, part schnauzer, can be very stubborn. So I did the only practical thing I could think of. I caved completely.

As soon as they put King Arthur in the carrier and the carrier into my hand, Ginny stood up and trotted alongside me without coaxing. Why not? She'd gotten her own way again. That's how King Arthur joined the family.

Strangely enough, that cat used the litter box at my house from day one. I thought about it and came to the conclusion that, because the family who took him had no other cats, King Arthur had no cat behavior to imitate. With all the cats I have doing the same thing in the litter box, he got the idea immediately. He's a highly intelligent animal.

At first, King Arthur was his old familiar self, the bully. He snarled and hissed at my other cats and intimidated them. They all began hiding, avoiding him at mealtime, so King Arthur was able to go from dish to dish, helping himself to whatever he wanted while the other cats trembled under the furniture. I had to feed them separately, after the big bully had filled his belly. I hoped that the passage of time would solve the King Arthur problem.

One day, shortly after he arrived at my house, King Arthur went one step too far. He picked on Madame. He hissed and spit at her, growling and snarling. But Madame is stone deaf and heard none of it. All she knew was that this strange cat was up in her face. Calmly, she lifted one dainty paw and bopped him, hard. King Arthur blinked and took two steps back. He sat down, thinking it over, and made another mistake. Getting up, he put himself in Madame's face for a second go-around. Once again she cuffed him, boxing his ears. This time he backed down for good.

Every bully is a coward, and King Arthur is no exception. Seeing this, my cats said to one another, "Hey, look, this guy isn't so tough! He's nothing but a wimp!" Once the cats had his number they stopped being afraid, and stood up to King Arthur whenever he opened his mouth to growl. King Arthur, being no dope, soon gave up his antisocial behavior and settled down into domesticity. He gets along with all the cats now, but he's still scared stiff of Madame and makes wide circles around her, just to be on the safe side. He's not hungry for another knuckle sandwich.

VINOLA

Vinola is named for a good friend of mine who, when she was alive, fed and rescued cats, just as Ginny and I do. She had 140 cats living with her; in my last book I called her "Ramona," to protect her privacy. But Vinola passed away in August of 1995, so I can now call her by her real name.

Madame knows that in an earlier life she was Queen Nefertiti of Egypt.

After she died, sixty-five of her cats went to upstate New York and the remainder were released back into the streets, where they are fed twice a day.

The cat Vinola, too, was an outside cat, and a very young one, perhaps four months old at the most. She was very friendly, even a little needy, always begging for attention and affection. Whenever I fed her, she simply jumped up into my arms.

My friend Phyllis Levy was born on October 4, the Feast of St. Francis, which may account for her deep compassion for helpless animals. When I told Phyllis about Vinola, and how she always jumped into my arms, Phyllis's eyes filled up with tears.

"Oh, Philip, can't you see what she's trying to tell you? She desperately wants to come home with you. Now I know what I want for my birthday. I want you to give Vinola a home."

How could I refuse a request like that? I know that Phyllis had only love in her heart when she interceded for Vinola, so I made her a promise. I was happy to make the sweet little cat another member of the Gonzalez family. And I turned out to be the winner, because Vinola is the most affectionate pet in the world.

By now I know my dog pretty well, and I can give you a list of the top five things she loves: Number one is me and Sheilah, her "daddy" and "mommy"; number two is the cats; number three is small children; number four is delicatessen, especially baked salmon; and number five is everybody else in the entire world, people and animals alike (except for some dogs).

Ginny is an affection junkie who lives to give affection as

well as accept it. She's my "love mop." You'd think that with a family of two humans and nineteen cats, all of whom adore her, she'd be satisfied. You'd be wrong. Add the huge extended family of cats we find and feed and sometimes find homes for, and that's at least eighty to one hundred more cats to love. But that's still not enough. Sometimes I think that Ginny won't be satisfied until she's licked every face in the world and groomed every cat. Children are especially high on her list.

On October 25, 1995, the Long Island newspaper *Newsday* ran a long feature story about Ginny and her remarkable rescues, Sheilah, and me. The article, written by a young intern named Matt Villano (his first big story), focused on Ginny's remarkable rescue of the Chairman from his prison of broken glass. The paper printed some wonderful photographs, including one, on the front page of its second section, of Ginny cuddling and grooming the little Chairman. It was read all over the Island, and brought many phone calls and letters to Ginny in care of the newspaper. Best of all, it brought a flood of donations to help in Ginny's rescues. We made a lot of new friends.

Shortly after the *Newsday* piece appeared, Matt Villano called me up to tell me that Mrs. Lara Davidson, a teacher at a school in Richmond Hill, Queens, was eager to get in touch with me. She had read Matt's article out loud to her class of fourth graders. When I phoned her, Mrs. Davidson told me that her students loved the story and all of them wanted to meet Ginny. Would we be willing to come to her school?

Would Ginny like to go to a place where little children would pet her and make a fuss over her? You couldn't keep her away! Sheilah had a special cake baked for the occasion, with Ginny's picture on it, just like the cover of the book. We decided to tell the children that it was Ginny's birthday, which wasn't exactly a fib because nobody knows exactly when she was born, although her official birthday is now the same as mine, April 1. Besides, any day that Ginny can be with children is exactly like a birthday party for her.

Mrs. Davidson's husband Adam picked Ginny and me up and drove us to P.S. 34 in Richmond Hill, to class 4-01. We brought two cats along with us, the Chairman and Sweet Pea. When we arrived at the school, Matt Villano, the *Newsday* reporter, was waiting for us.

Let me tell you a little about Sweet Pea. There was a litter of kittens, about six weeks old, that we fed at the site near the animal shelter where Ken Colon works. Someone had just dumped the mother and her kittens there. I named them Tessa, Maxine, Bad Mike, and Sweet Pea. One day we found Sweet Pea, the smallest of the litter, running back and forth, crying. We couldn't tell what was wrong with her, and because she was trapped behind the fence that closed in the parking lot of the Airtite Window factory, we couldn't get to her. So I asked Kenny to catch her for me, and I'd take her to the vet.

Sweet Pea gave Kenny a hard time, but eventually he managed to get hold of her. There was nothing seriously wrong with her, but she did have infected eyes, worms, and sores all over her. When we got her cleaned up and healed, she was adorable. So after she had her shots I decided to take her along to the school together with the Chairman for "show and tell." I wanted the children to see for themselves the kind of animals who can be rescued from the streets with a little sympathy and kindness. And Sweet Pea was so cute and friendly I was hoping somebody at the school would melt and give her a home.

As soon as my dog set a paw into the classroom, the kids went wild. "Ginny!" they yelled, as though greeting a hero. "Ginny! Over here, Ginny! I love you, Ginny!"

Ginny smiled all over her face as the children began touching and patting her. She didn't know where to start first, and her tail was wagging so hard I was afraid it would lift her off the ground like a helicopter rotor. She walked around the classroom and kissed all the kids happily. There were about forty students, and their desks were arranged in one large horseshoe, with Ginny in the middle as the center of attention, just as she likes it. To show the students how docile she was, Ginny dropped to her belly and did a minute of the famous Ginny Crawl, which made the children laugh. Only one of the children seemed to be afraid of Ginny, but when my dog crawled toward her with that imploring look in her eyes, the little girl lost her fear.

While we were there, Mrs. Davidson held the Chairman for about an hour while the students held little Sweet Pea, petting her and passing her around from hand to hand. Then they switched, and the Chairman got passed around while Sweet Pea stayed in the teacher's lap. Both cats enjoyed the human contact very much; besides, with Ginny in the same room they knew they had nothing to fear.

When I began to talk to the children about Ginny, telling them how I found her in the shelter (or, rather, how she found me) and how she began to rescue cats, the kids were as quiet as mice, and their eyes were large with amazement. They'd never heard anything like this before, yet here was the wonder dog herself, sitting right there in front of them in their own classroom. This was an abused animal who had been abandoned, but who survived into a wonderful life where her affection and her remarkable gifts were appreciated. Ginny was like a living lesson in fur, a lesson that kindness and caring can work miracles. It was also the first time any of them had ever seen a real-life hero.

I told the eager children about how Ginny was locked in a closet when her owner moved out, left to starve and die, and how the shelter had brought her back to life and put her up for adoption. I admitted to them that I didn't want to take her at first, but that little dog looked at me in such a special way that I fell in love with her. I told them about a few of her remarkable rescues, including her discovery of a litter of five newborn kittens in a large pipe, how she found the two little tuxedos, Black and White, under a junked car, how she saved the Chairman from a box full of broken glass, and how she cut her paws but paid no attention to her pain.

I could see that the children were impressed, not only with Ginny, but with the kittens they'd been petting, Sweet Pea and the Chairman. Here were survivors, and they were happy and healthy—all through kindness and the desire to make a difference, just like Ginny herself. The kids had food for thought here; it made me very glad that we could be good examples for them.

When I finished talking, many of the children had questions.

"How old are your cats?"

"How come you have so many cats?"

"Gee, I don't think that's so many. I'd love to have a lot more."

"Does anybody complain?" I had to confess that there are people who do complain about a large number of cats all together. These are people who don't understand how precious life is.

"How did you come to write the book?" I explained about the first article in *Good Housekeeping*, and how it led to the book.

"Are you gonna save all the cats in the world?"

I answered honestly, "I wish I could."

"Would you save any animal you came across?"

I had to think about that one. "I love all animals, and I would certainly try to help any animal in trouble, if it was in my power."

"Did Ginny go into the ocean to rescue that seal?"

"No, the seal came up on the shore, but Ginny didn't want to leave it, and really expected me to take it home."

"Seals bark. Do you think Ginny thought it was another dog?"

That had never occurred to me; kids are so smart. "Maybe. Maybe she did think it was a dog, a very big dog. But Ginny loves every creature in the world."

"Would you save a whale?"

"I would if I could, but I don't think I'd ever be called on to do it."

After the question and answer period, we had our "birthday" party. Mrs. Davidson's husband Adam had also brought a cake, so there was plenty to go around. Everyone sang "Happy Birthday" to Ginny, and we cut the cake. All the children had some, and so did Ginny, Mrs. Davidson, Matt, and I. Then they gave Ginny presents. A number of the children had brought cans of cat food and dog food for Ginny and the cats, and they gave them to us as Ginny's birthday presents. During the party we took photographs.

Mrs. Davidson was very interested in Sweet Pea, whom she'd been holding in her lap and petting. She felt a bond with the little thing. The next weekend, she and her husband came to my house and they adopted her. Unfortunately, Mr. Davidson is allergic to cats, and his allergies really kicked in, so they brought Sweet Pea back to me a month or so later. But she has a good home now, with a loving family. Sweet Pea was one of the three cats adopted on Christmas Eve.

Ginny was reluctant to leave her new young friends, but as we were heading out the door, another teacher stopped us and invited us into her classroom so that her students, too, could see Ginny. Ginny led the way eagerly, and made another group of children happy. Before we left the school, the students of Mrs. Davidson's 4-01 class gave us a poster they had made showing Ginny under printed headlines like "Ginny, Hero" and "We Love Ginny."

The following month I received a stack of letters and drawings—of cats, Ginny, and even me—from another class of fourth graders and a kindergarten class, both from the Fayette School in North Merrick, Long Island.

Dear Mr. Gonzalez:

We read the article about you in *Newsday*. We were deeply touched to hear about what you've done to help animals in need.

Enclosed are drawings from the students in Mrs. Bird's kindergarten and letters from Ms. Hunt's fourth grade class. Our letters and pictures explain what we have done to help you continue your work. We hope you enjoy perusing what we have sent you!!

Sincerely,
Mrs. Bird
Ms. Hunt

The children wrote wonderful letters; I keep them and prize them. Zachary, who signed himself "always kind to animals," was concerned about Ginny's paws, cut by the broken glass in the Chairman rescue. Fahim told me he was "dedicated to animals," and advised me and Ginny to go out and find more cats to help. Tommy wanted to know if it was boring not being able to go to work. (No, Tommy, because cat rescue *is* my work, and it's full-time and never boring.) Bianca wrote me that she had a cat named Misha and, "I never liked dogs but if I met Ginny, I think I would like her."

Included with the letters was a check. The children had raised the money by holding a two-day bake sale (Fahim wrote me that they had eaten the leftover brownies), and they wanted to put the money to use helping animals. When their teacher, Ms. Hunt, read her class the newspaper article about

Ginny, they decided to send the bake sale money to Ginny to help with our rescue efforts and buy food for our stray cats.

The children were eager to meet Ginny and me, and invited us to their classroom, so once again I took Ginny to school. Before the day we were supposed to go, Ginny dug out the little tuxedo cat from under the grass and sod in the landscaping truck, so I named the kitten Ms. Hunt in honor of the Merrick teacher. I wanted to bring a cat or kitten along with us to show the children a living example of one of Ginny's rescues, just as I'd done for P.S. 34, but my arm was really hurting that day and Ginny was about all I could manage. So it would have to be just the two of us.

The husband of Mrs. Bird, the kindergarten teacher, picked us up and brought us to the Fayette School. We got to the school at nine in the morning. Instead of going to a classroom, we were brought into the auditorium, which held enough seats for two classes of children. The school principal was there to greet us, and the children began filing in. When they spotted Ginny, they called out to her, and it was hard to tell who was more enthusiastic, the kids or Ginny. She went wild, kissing and licking faces, and the children couldn't get enough of petting her. At last they sat down, but they were still excited.

I was given a microphone, the first time in my life I'd ever used one. I brought with me photographs of Ginny and her cats, and I handed them out to the children. Once again I told the story of my dog and her miraculous rescues, about the disabled and abused cats who drew Ginny to them like magnets, and about how she finds them in the darndest places, where nobody else—human or animal—could possibly find them. How she does this nobody understands, I told them.

The children listened with full attention, never taking their eyes off Ginny. As I talked about her, I could see from their faces that the children were really thinking about Ginny's rescues, and about the importance of being kind to animals. They had lots of questions when I finished, and I answered them the best way I could.

One little kindergarten boy (I think his name was Tommy) told me he knew me. When I asked him how he knew me, he answered that his mother had read him the book that "Ginny wrote," and that he knew she'd saved me as well as cats. It felt great to realize that here was a kid who knew my story and Ginny's from *The Dog Who Rescues Cats*.

It was now about 10:30, and I'd been there ninety minutes. It was time for us to leave and for the children to go to their classes, although we were reluctant to part with one another. The children especially didn't want to say good-bye to Ginny. One fourth grader asked me for a photo of myself to put into his album of sports stars and heroes. He said I was a hero to him, and that made me *feel* like a hero.

Recently, we were invited by Dr. Gelfand, our veterinarian, to go to the Lakeside School, where the vet's son Alexander is a third grader. We were going to have yet another "birthday party" for Ginny, so we ordered another cake with Ginny's picture on it, and I bought candy and soft drinks.

Dr. Gelfand arranged to pick us up; when he arrived, I called him out of his car so that he could give me a hand carrying the Chairman, who was also a guest of honor. Children always love the Chairman because his rescue from the broken glass is so thrilling. Whenever I tell them that story, they listen with all their attention, sitting on the edges of their chairs. They gasp and they smile and they think Ginny is the biggest, bravest hero in the world. Needless to say, I quite agree with them.

So the doctor and I came out in the building hall, ready to go. But Ginny was so excited that she was dancing around, and accidentally pushed the door shut behind us. Now my keys and Ginny were locked inside, together with the cake and other snacks. Sensing that something was wrong, Ginny started barking her head off.

What to do? My apartment door is a strong, metal door and its only weak point is the doorknob, which is drilled through the metal. So I took a few steps back and began to kick the door, again and again. Maybe because Ginny and I walk so much, my legs are pretty strong. Each time I kicked, Ginny would bark louder. At last, after ten or a dozen powerful kicks, the doorknob gave way and I was able to get the door open. There was a dead bolt, so I could relock the door before we left. In New York City, you don't leave your apartment unprotected, and Long Island is close enough to be New York.

By the time we loaded Ginny, the refreshments, and the Chairman into Dr. Gelfand's car, we had got a late start. The third graders and their teacher Mrs. Lenore Smiley were waiting patiently for us, sitting quietly on their best behavior. But the instant they saw Ginny, everybody went nuts. The kids began to yell for her, and Ginny, as usual when she sees children, was in ecstasy, going from one child to another, getting hugs and giving kisses. Ginny soaks up all the affection just like a sponge mop. Children and dog were so excited it took us a few minutes to calm everybody down.

First Dr. Gelfand talked about Ginny and her remarkable rescues. Then I told them how Ginny became my dog, and how she changed my life. After that, I gave them the story of Ginny's strange and angelic love for cats, and how she rescues them in every kind of circumstance. I could see that these wonderful third graders were really getting our message of respect for life and kindness to helpless animals. They could see with their own eyes that the dog and the little cat Chairman were shining examples of how human kindness can pay off in love.

One little girl was allergic to cats, and Mrs. Smiley tried to isolate her from Ginny, telling her to go and sit at the back of the room.

"No, I said I was allergic to *cats,* not *dogs!*" she protested, and ran to give Ginny a big hug and a kiss.

The kids had loads of questions for Dr. Gelfand and me, and we answered as many as possible, but time was running short. After we sang "Happy Birthday" to Ginny, the third time she's heard it in as many months, we had to leave. The third graders were scheduled for another activity in another classroom and our lateness had cut into their time. We left the uncut cake and all the other treats behind for the kids, who hated to see Ginny go, probably almost as much as Ginny hated to leave her beloved children. Going to visit classes at our local schools has turned into one of Ginny's favorite playtime activities. Her "birthday parties" are as much of a celebration for her as they are for the children.

I don't know who gets more inspiration out of my school visits: the children, Ginny, or me. But I'd bet you twenty bucks it's me.

Mookie in a pensive mood.

Dottie checking you out.

Caesar gets forty winks.

Madame in her world of silence.

Tiger: bigger than a breadbox.

Some of our indoor cats.

CHAPTER 4

THE STORM OF THE CENTURY

*T*HAT SUNDAY MORNING EARLY IN JANUARY, Sheilah, Ginny, and I got a late start in feeding the cats. The sun was already high and the day, although very cold, was sunny and clear. As we moved from one feeding station to the next, the street cats and kittens all came running out to meet us, cold and hungry because their breakfast was late. There was a lot of impatient mewing and grateful rubbing against our legs, a combination of "Hurry up!" and "Thank you."

All the weather predictions we'd heard were for a snowstorm later in the day, so we brought a lot of extra cat food with us, just in case we couldn't get back through the snow for the night feeding, and we filled the bowls to overflowing. Before we reached the last of the feeding stations, the sunny sky had turned gray and the first snow was starting to fall. The flakes were huge, and they fell thickly, beginning almost immediately to stick to the ground.

Ginny loves cold and snow; she is part Siberian husky, and has a thick coat. Snow is her element. She can hardly wait for winter to come every year. As the flakes fell on her face and stuck to her fur, a big smile appeared on her face and she began to bark. I know that bark. It signals "play-time," so I knew that Ginny was looking forward to romping in the snowdrifts, rolling and digging. But I was worried about the cats. Snow is very bad news for homeless animals who have no shelter to count on. I didn't realize it right then, but Ginny and I were about to face the greatest challenge we would meet since we began our rescue of homeless cats.

By the time we'd fed the last group of cats and turned to go home, the snow was falling thickly and quickly. Already, an inch or two had accumulated, and we couldn't see twenty feet ahead of us. We knew we were in for a big one, but we didn't know then that this blizzard would go into the record books as "the Storm of the Century."

The Blizzard of 1996

By seven o'clock that evening, about eighteen inches had fallen, and there was no letup in sight. The storm was the lead and almost the only story on both the local and the national TV news; none of the forecasters seemed to know when it would stop, or how much snow we'd finally be left with. Guesses ranged from eighteen inches to thirty-six. Thirty-six inches of snow? That was three feet of the stuff, so much snow the outdoor animals would literally be buried. All I could think about was those poor cats out in the street. What would happen to them? How would they survive?

Storm or no storm, I made up my mind to go out again and feed them. Even though we had left that extra food out for the cats, I was afraid that the bowls might be covered over in snow, or maybe they'd frozen into solid ice. The cats might be waiting for us at the feeding stations, out in the bitter cold and biting snow, from hunger and force of habit. I didn't think it was fair to ask Sheilah to take her car out on a night like this. Besides, all the TV and radio news broadcasters were urgently warning motorists to stay off the roads except in cases of emergency.

So I took down some cans of food and heated them in a sink full of hot water, then I put them in a pail together with dry food. I could manage a pail with one hand, even if it was pretty heavy. Ginny and I went out on foot, out into the terrible weather. It was still snowing very hard. Thanks to the high winds that came with the storm, much of the snow on the ground had drifted into tall banks. Some of the drifts were over Ginny's head, but the Siberian husky blood in her veins saw those snowdrifts as a great opportunity for having fun. She would dive into them headfirst, rolling around in the snow and digging big holes whenever I'd let her. But tonight I wasn't very patient with her need to play. I was interested only in getting to the hungry cats.

"Ginny, come on! Hurry up!" I urged her again and again. But she was hard to convince.

Slowly we made our way to the three feeding stations nearest to my home, but there were no cats in sight. I figured they were taking shelter from the storm, but where? I called out to them and waited, but we saw no cats. I have to admit I was pretty worried, especially about the other five feeding stations I couldn't get to on foot. I could picture the poor animals hanging around, freezing cold and wet to the bone, waiting for their dinner. Or hiding where I couldn't find them, thinking hungrily about Iams and Fancy Feast.

I decided then and there that this *was* an emergency, and I went home and knocked on Sheilah's door. When it comes to saving cats, nobody is more eager than Sheilah, so she went out and dug her car out from under a pile of snow and off we went. I arranged the cans of food on the dashboard and put the dry food sack on the floor by my feet, then I fiddled with the vents, diverting the warm air coming in through them in order to heat the food up. I turned the dashboard into a kind of Primus stove.

With snow swirling everywhere, cutting visibility to zero, and the roads icy under our tires, driving was very difficult. Many roads were simply closed, and we had to detour over and over. Also, we got stuck several times, and it took a lot of wheel-spinning and motor-gunning to start the Camry up again. But with all that, we did manage to get to every one of our feeding areas.

All in all we saw only four cats. Two were in the feeding

station we call Shelter or the Maxines, and there we saw only Maxine and Beige. Two were at Ruby's, and we fed Ruby and Co Co. At last we turned around and went home, worried and anxious about the others, more than seventy-five of them. In weather as cold as this, homeless animals need even more food than usual, as calories to use as fuel to help keep them warm. These animals ate only what we fed them, and were accustomed to eating twice a day every day. I didn't sleep well that night, I can tell you.

My indoor cats—Tiger, Spot, Caesar, Dottie, Sasha, Cali, the Chairman, Solomon, Napoleon, Darlene, Madame, Rosie, King Arthur, Vinola, Revlon, Clippie, Tulip, and Blondie—were fascinated by the falling snow. They did nothing but sit at the windows, watching the swirling flakes with full attention and a look of wonder. They would run from window to window, nudging one another out of the way to get a better view. They'd never seen a snowfall as heavy as this one.

By the time we went out again, 4:30 Monday morning, the storm was tapering off, having left about two feet of snow behind on the ground, and much higher drifts by the curbsides. We dressed very warmly. I was lucky enough to receive a really great down coat as a Christmas present, a joint gift from Cleveland Amory, Phyllis Levy, and Phyllis's friend Marion Finger. I wore that with thick gloves. The coat is like a blast furnace, good for weather down to seventy degrees below zero, and it kept me so warm it was like August inside. Sheilah was bundled up in her warmest coat, her head muffled in a scarf and a hat, her hands in warm gloves. As for Ginny, she was dressed only in her own fur, which is very thick and warm. Being part husky, she doesn't feel the cold. She has sweaters and even little jackets, some of them gifts from her fans, but she doesn't like to wear them, and kicks up a fuss when I try to put them on her.

This time it took Sheilah more than an hour to get her Camry dug out, but at last we set off, with pails of hot water, sacks of dry food, and cans getting warm on the dashboard "stove." We went looking for hungry cats, but we didn't see any.

When we got to Ruby's feeding station, Ginny ran out of the car and dashed over to one of the parked cars. It was buried so deeply in snow that you could barely make out the outline of the vehicle. Ginny began to dig ferociously, barking at me to come and help. I joined her and began to dig also, and there, under the snowed-in car, we found three little cats, two black and one gray. Their names were Athos, Porthos, and Aramis, after the Three Musketeers, and they were very young. I was feeling quite pleased with myself, and as usual very proud of Ginny, because we probably just saved three lives, but when I walked around the car I saw that there was an opening in the snow there, and the cats could have gotten out by themselves if they'd wanted to. I took a hard look at Ginny and she was giving me a big, broad grin. I realized that she only wanted us to dig in the snow together; it was her idea of a winter game. Nevertheless, she knew there were cats under that car, and as usual I had no idea how she knew. We saw only one more cat, a strange white cat with black patches that at first I thought were his markings, but which later turned out to be tar. With Athos, Porthos, and Aramis, I just had to name the new one D'Artagnan, so I did.

We were scheduled to feed in the evening as well, but many streets were closed and even blocked off because they hadn't been cleaned yet by the Long Beach snowplows. Getting to the feeding stations in the dark posed a real logistical problem for us. Then the telephone calls began to come.

We didn't realize just how many good friends we had until we really needed them. Sheilah had made a wide acquaintance among animal lovers who'd met her while she was feeding cats at the three areas furthest from the house. People telephoned her from those areas to tell us that we shouldn't try to get to those stations tonight, and that they would cover them and feed our street cats for us. We accepted gratefully, and a small army of volunteers made certain that none of the cats who showed up went hungry.

We did go out that night, of course, and got to those five feeding stations we were able to reach without too much trouble. At our 7 P.M. feeding on Monday, we saw and fed only six cats, but six were better than four, and I was beginning to have hope that my street guys had survived.

I still kept my "motel" open on my terrace, hoping that a number of the outside cats would find their way up there for shelter and food. Amanda and Eugene were the only ones who came, and Amanda would sleep in one of the cat "rooms," although Eugene would only stop long enough to eat and then disappear back into the snowy street.

The Blizzard of 1996 made headlines all over the country. Washington, New York, Boston, and cities in Pennsylvania came to an absolute standstill. Schools and shops were closed; people couldn't get to work; and even the post office, whose motto is "Neither snow, nor rain, nor heat, nor gloom of night shall stay these couriers from the swift completion of their appointed rounds," had to give in to *this* snow. There were no mail deliveries. You couldn't turn on the TV without seeing wide expanses of brilliant white. Cars were buried and all but invisible; nothing was moving except a few brave people on foot and some emergency vehicles, all of which were having a rough go of it.

News reporters with camcorders were out there, dressed in parkas with their hoods up, interviewing men and women on skis in the middle of Fifth Avenue; three guys came all the way down from upstate New York on snowmobiles. When they got to the city, they made the evening news and the front pages, everybody took their pictures, and the cops gave them a ticket. People were smiling and cheerful and making the best of it, but all I could think of was the homeless cats and the effect the storm would be having on them. Reporters were covering homeless people, who were provided with shelters. Rescue workers were looking for stranded motorists and checking on elderly people to make sure they had sufficient heat and food. But nobody in the media ever seems to talk about homeless animals in terrible weather. Cats and dogs don't make the six o'clock news.

Even on Tuesday, after the snow plows and sanders came through, the snow was piled up at the curbs three feet high and higher. The Long Island Railroad wasn't running, and my little windswept ocean-front town was practically cut off from the rest of the world. Police were still stopping any vehicles daring to drive through the streets; only genuine emergency workers were allowed to use their cars to get to work. But there weren't many vehicles; most of them were still at the curbs, buried under two feet of snow.

It was very rough going because of the ice underfoot. The cold winds off the Atlantic Ocean turned the sidewalks to sheets of ice, and even my good boots, which have excellent traction, weren't quite good enough. Ginny and I went slipping and sliding all along our route.

On Tuesday morning after the Sunday-to-Monday blizzard we fed twenty-three cats who crept out toward us, wet, shivering, starved. By the Tuesday evening feeding there were, thank God, fifty desperate cats meowing hungrily for food. They were beginning to come out of their makeshift shelters, probably under cars and trucks, in doorways and cellar openings, and anywhere a small flexible body can wiggle in to get out of the worst of the weather. But we were still close to thirty cats short of our usual number, and I was determined to find them. As much as I worried about them, I knew that my Ginny's own private radar could be trusted to locate them.

THE SWIMMING POOL RESCUE

That same evening Ginny, Sheilah, and I went out looking for missing cats. Near one of our feeding stations there was a large house with a swimming pool where we found cats from time to time and fed them. Ginny wanted to look there; her barks and her body language told me so.

We went over to the yard with the pool to see what we could, and no cats were visible. But Ginny pointed her nose and her entire body at the pool and went on barking. I decided to take the risk myself. It was pretty dark out, but I was still nervous. I knew that the house and the pool belonged to a man who really hated cats. I didn't want him to find out that cats were hanging around his house, because I don't put it past him to poison them to get rid of them. This was the same guy who pushed my friend Vinola when she was out feeding strays, even though she was over seventy years old. So I decided not to involve Sheilah or Ginny. Besides, I would have to trespass on private property, and that should be my decision alone.

I handed Ginny's leash to Sheilah and told them to stay behind. Taking my stick with me, I snuck past the tall wooden fence around the property and made for the pool. It was one of those large above-ground swimming pools, with metal mesh fencing around the base of it. Ginny barked louder and more quickly, as though telling me that I was getting warm.

I began to dig a hole through the hard frozen snow around the mesh and, as soon as I broke through, I peeped in and saw them. Seven cats, all huddled together for warmth under the pool, behind the snow. They'd been trapped there, snowed in, probably for three days. The snow had provided them with water to drink, but they'd had no food. The frozen snow had afforded them protection and some shelter from the wind, and probably kept them minimally warm. The Inuits of Alaska live in homes made of blocks of snow, and the snow insulates them from the cold. Maybe the snow even saved the cats' lives.

Anyway, as soon as they saw the hole and me, those cats popped out one by one. I counted Joanie, Izzy, and Ferdinand, all of whom came from the same litter. They were followed by Freyo, Vito, Bobbie, and the Godfather. All of them ran out to Ginny and Sheilah and, of course, to the food that they knew we had brought them. They were so skinny it would break your heart to see them, obviously starving. We gave them a large meal hot from the dashboard, some fresh clean water, and we left them there, free to take shelter again. I hated to leave them, wondering how they'd protect themselves from the cold.

Even when the snow was largely cleared, feeding the cats became something of a hazard because of the heavy ice underfoot and especially on the roadways. Just keeping my balance was a twice-daily problem. One day, when I was out feeding with Ginny and one of Sheilah's volunteers, a car came around the corner doing sixty miles an hour and hit a patch of ice. It skidded, fishtailed around, and came heading straight for us, out of control. I moved fast, grabbing the volunteer with my one good hand and pushing both of us out of the way of the wheels. We just made it by a whisker, and the car sped off again without stopping. Why anybody would drive at that speed in icy conditions is beyond me; it might have resulted in a tragedy instead of just a scary incident.

When all was said and done, the only one who thoroughly enjoyed the blizzard and its frozen aftermath was my Ginny. At least ten times a day she forced me out of the house for a romp in the snow. She runs around like crazy, and throws herself into the snowdrifts. She makes trails. With my left hand I make snowballs and throw them for her, and she runs to fetch them back. Some of them she even catches in her mouth, like a Frisbee, leaping up to get them in her teeth.

One of the street cats whom we feed at the Paradise feeding station also likes cold and snow. Whenever Van Gogh saw Ginny she ran after her and jumped up on her for a ride, and they'd play together. But what Ginny seems to enjoy most is trying to push me down into the snow. She jumps up on me and pushes hard with her paws, hoping to get me off balance. Sometimes I'd let myself fall down deliberately, and sometimes she was successful in knocking me down all by herself, using only her strength and enthusiasm. I think she wants to bring me down to her size, so we can be two playful dogs together, rolling around in a snowdrift.

BEIGE AT SEA

After the snow and the ice came the thaw, and the thaw brought major flooding. Not only water from the melting snow but from the ocean itself flooded into Long Beach's streets and basements, forming large lakes here and there. A lot of the cats were missing again, cut off by the large pools of water. They were hiding out, but they couldn't get to the feeding stations. Cars couldn't get through, but I went mushing in icy water up to my knees in search of cats to feed.

The only one I saw was Beige, near the area where the

Rosie has the sweetest expression, almost as sweet as she is.

glass factory trucks are parked, where Ginny found the Chairman buried under all that broken glass. Beige was floating on a large deep puddle of water, as big as a small pond, clinging to what looked like the lid of a plastic garbage can. She was right in the middle of the puddle, too far from either shore to jump to safety. The poor cat was disoriented and absolutely terrified, hissing with fear, her eyes wide and her ears laid back on her head. How did she ever get herself into such a predicament?

As soon as she saw Beige, Ginny started to dash into the water, which was deep enough to be over her head.

"No, Ginny! Come back!" I yelled, and I yanked hard on her leash. As soon as I had her safe, I picked Ginny up and locked her into the car.

I knew that my dog could swim, but I was afraid that the water was too cold even for her, and I was anxious, too, because Beige was so scared I thought she might take a swipe at Ginny with her claws. As I saw it, the smart thing to do was not to try to get her at all, but to somehow maneuver her garbage-lid raft to the edge of the deep pool so that she could jump to dry land. I took the stick I carry for moving the food bowls, and I kept poking at her garbage lid. It moved, but only a little, not enough to get her to safety. So I bit the bullet and waded in myself.

The water was even colder than I imagined, and it soon covered my boot tops and crept up my legs. My teeth began to chatter so loudly I could hear them over Ginny's excited barking. I moved closer and poked harder. Like a boat at sea, the garbage lid went sailing over the huge puddle until it almost reached the far side. Beige took one mighty jump and made it safely to shore. The minute she was on dry land she lost all her fear, and came trotting around the side of the puddle toward Ginny, anxious to be fed.

Another thing that gave me trouble during the winter of '96 was the cats' food bowls. A long time ago, I switched over from cheap, lightweight bowls to heavier stoneware bowls, which cost me about four dollars each. At least they wouldn't blow away in a high wind. I would collect them with every feeding and bring them home to be washed, leaving fresh ones behind.

Those good stoneware bowls were too much of a temptation to some really uncaring and greedy people. They began to disappear; there were fewer and fewer of them left every time we came back to the feeding stations. Sometimes I'd find piles of cat food where somebody had actually dumped the food on the ground to get at the bowls.

So, even though they were less satisfactory, plastic bowls had to be the answer. I buy them in large quantities from a liquidator for about eighty cents each, but there are problems with them, too. They're not as sturdy as stoneware, and they can blow away in windy weather, which we had had a lot of recently. Also, we began finding a lot of them broken, and there were rocks all around them. So I think that some people—possibly kids—were throwing rocks at the cats while they were eating. I wish I could catch them at it. I'm keeping my eyes open for anybody with a rock in his hand and a mean expression on his face.

We never missed one feeding time in all the days during and after the Blizzard of 1996; even when the cats didn't show up, we did. And, when it was all back to normal and we did a head count, we had lost only one cat, Scarlett. But there really was no "only" about it; a lost cat is a lost cat, and not one of them can be spared. I looked high and low for her, my heart in my mouth, but without success.

On February 1, weeks later, who should show up to be fed but Scarlett! That made me feel so good, even though she was wretched-looking, emaciated, and weak. But they had all survived, every one of them. I had the sudden desire to go out and have eighty tiny T-shirts made up with the slogan "I Survived the '96 Blizzard, and All I Got from Philip Was This Lousy T-shirt" printed on them. When I pictured eighty cats running around Long Beach with little shirts on I laughed my head off.

But the idea of homeless animals in rough winters is far from a laughing matter. Ginny and I have eight feeding stations, but sometimes I think eight million feeding stations would barely be enough to save the lives of all the stray animals who need our help in order to survive. I cover my small corner of the world to the best of my ability, with the help of very good friends and with all my heart. I wish I could count our rescues in the tens of thousands. I wonder how many animals suffered and died in the Blizzard of 1996, and how many were swept away to drown in the floods that followed it? We'll never know.

As far as I'm concerned, the only answer is spaying or neutering. When I freed those seven cats from under the swimming pool, I noticed that they were all cats I'd taken to the veterinarian and had neutered. So, although they were huddled together, male and female alike, no unwanted kittens were going to be born in the next nine weeks. Often, people begrudge spending the money to neuter their pets. When the kittens start to arrive, they put them into shelters or, much worse, they throw them away like garbage into the streets, abandoning them to injury, disease, and death, and contributing to the mounting crisis of unwanted animals.

The great Blizzard of 1996 forced me to reexamine a problem I'd always had to deal with: the problem of providing shelter from the cold for my street cats. In the past, I'd fallen back on makeshift arrangements that worked most of the time. Sheilah and I wrapped heavy plastic bags around cardboard cartons and left them out as shelters against rain, wind, and cold. It was a kind of pussycat shantytown, but it did the trick for a while. The cats used the cartons, but the vacant lots we left the boxes on weren't ours, and we didn't really have the legal right to erect cat shelters on other peoples' property. The owners of the land complained, so the boxes had to be removed.

But the winter of 1996 was so severe that no number of cardboard cartons, not even cartons protected by plastic bags and lined in old clothes and towels, would have provided adequate shelter. Boxes would blow away in weather like this; they wouldn't stand a chance. Bringing dangerous and record-breaking cold to the Midwest, 1996 was the coldest winter since the U.S. Weather Service began keeping records. On February 2 in Tower, Minnesota, the mercury dropped to sixty below zero, the coldest in Minnesota history; the old record, set ninety years ago, was fifty below. In Wisconsin, farm animals were freezing to death, and all over dairy country ears and tails were freezing and breaking off newborn calves. Hell froze over—as the town of Hell, Michigan, became a sheet of ice. Chicago was freezing so badly that people were dying. Texas, Louisiana, and Oklahoma suffered under icy conditions and the roads were so slippery that automobiles piled up in multivehicle accidents. Even the usually warm and sunny south was clobbered by snow and ice; states like Florida, Mississippi, Georgia, Kentucky, and Tennessee weren't ready for weather conditions like these. From what the weather projections, predictions, and guesses by meteorologists tell us, thanks to global warming, future winters look to be as hard as 1996, maybe even harder. Who, I wonder, will shelter homeless cats?

As I walked through the snow, I gave this a lot of thought, and I'm still agonizing over it. I've lost a lot of sleep. Ideally, I'd like to buy a small piece of property near my house, just for the use of the cats, and erect permanent shelters for them, windproof, waterproof, and warm enough to keep out the worst of the cold. But I don't have the means to do that, and I'm not up on what the zoning laws in my little town permit or prohibit. I know there would be loud complaints from some of my neighbors.

Maybe I could find some run-down building to use, but I'm sure that some cat-hating people living nearby would call the health department, even though Sheilah and I would keep the facility clean. All I know is that I'm now as determined to bring shelter to my outdoor cats as I am to bring them food. Ginny and I don't want to see them suffer next winter as we did this one. I have to figure the whole thing out, but I will. I think about it all the time.

One of our outdoor cats, D'Artagnan, enjoying the shade of a table.

CHAPTER 5

FEEDING STATIONS AND LOOKOUTS

*A*S YOU KNOW, GINNY, SHEILAH, AND I go out to feed homeless cats every morning and every evening, seven days a week. I can reach three of the dinner stations on foot, carrying everything I need in one plastic supermarket bag, but most of the time we travel from feeding spot to feeding spot in Sheilah's Camry, which allows us to carry a large load of food, filtered water, and clean bowls. We have two large, clean garbage pails. One is filled with cans of food and the other comes back with the dirty cat dishes. A basket holds bottles of clean water and clean feeding dishes.

We usually tote this load in the trunk of the car, except on windy days. When the wind blows hard, it brings the trunk door crashing down on my head as I lift the food out of the trunk. I see stars. That trunk door has gotten me several times and even bopped Sheilah once or twice. So on windy days the supplies ride in the backseat, next to Ginny.

We drive very slowly, especially at night, because Sheilah is mortally terrified of hitting a cat. When they hear us coming (and they seem to recognize the sound of Sheilah's Camry) a lot of the cats come out to meet us, but they always stop before they get to the curb. Even so, Sheilah's always petrified that one or more of them will dash into the street and under our wheels, and no amount of reassurance on my part will convince her there's no chance of that happening. The cats are just too street-smart at the feeding stations, which is familiar territory. It's when they wander off to parts unknown that they sometimes get hit by cars.

Ginny sits in the backseat most of the time, but sometimes she'll jump in the front seat so she can see better (she's always got to know what's going on). When in front she sits on my lap and kind of supervises everything.

This routine is probably the single major factor of my life, and I love it, even in bad weather. Nothing gives me the satisfaction of seeing my outdoor cats chowing down with good appetite, nothing except finding good homes for them and bringing them in out of the cold. I have names for all my feeding stations, and names for all the outdoor cats who congregate there regularly, although new cats keep coming and going. Very recently, there's been an influx of solid black kittens. They're adorable, but there are an amazingly large number of them. I have no idea where they're coming from or who their parents might be (although my instincts tell me that one very active black tom is probably the father of them all by different mothers), but they have turned up at several of my feeding stations, and they do get fed. At any one given time, between eighty and one hundred cats get their breakfast and dinner from Ginny, Sheilah, and me. Feeding costs mount up to at least $800 a month and that doesn't include our veterinarian bills, which run to thousands of dollars a year.

For example, take Prince Philip. He's another great little cat who's unlucky enough to have FIV, feline AIDS. At this writing, Prince Philip has been at All Creatures for six months, at a cost of $9 a day. I love him too much to have him put to sleep, and I'm hoping that some good-hearted person will give him a home while he's still not too sick to enjoy it, as I have with Blondie. Meanwhile, we foot Prince Philip's bill as a necessary part of the work we do and hope for the best. At least we know he's getting the finest medical attention possible.

PARADISE AND OTTO

Paradise was one of our first locations, because it's just around the corner from where I live. When Ginny started me off on a life of rescuing, the natural place for me to start was Paradise, which is named not for its Garden of Eden qualities, but for the fact that a nursing home called Paradise used to exist nearby. There were always homeless cats hanging around there, and Ginny loved to romp with them and get me to feed them. Paradise is also a vacant lot where people go to walk their dogs. The dogs keep the stray cats at a distance, but not when Ginny is around. She won't stand for that. Even though she's smaller than a lot of the dogs who walk there, Ginny's bark is so commanding that it stops even the biggest dogs in their tracks. That bark says very clearly, "Cut that out! Now!" And they do. So the cats get to eat in peace.

The cats at Paradise are Van Gogh, Herod, Scarlett, and Carroll. Herod, Scarlett, and Carroll stay hidden; when they see us coming, out they pop. But Van Gogh is always waiting there for us, or, rather, for Ginny, whom she adores. Ginny is her favorite playmate.

There's another creature I feed at Paradise. It's a possum I named Otto. Sheilah doesn't want me feeding possums or raccoons; she's afraid more for the cats' sake than for mine, I think. But Otto never bothers the cats. Possums are very shy, and Otto is no exception. Nobody ever gets a glimpse of him except me. When Otto catches sight of me I swear he gives me a smile. He certainly recognizes me as the person with the food, and he thrives on cat food—Iams, Fancy Feast, and Whiskas. I don't go near him, though, because he is a wild creature. Both of us keep our distance, more acquaintances than friends.

KITTENS AND CATS

I think of the feeding station I named Kittens as my "artist's colony," because the baby cats who eat there are called Chagall, Picasso, Renoir, Dali, and Monet. They all hang out in the yard of a corner house about a block away from where I live. I suppose that I should move Van Gogh into this area, to keep all my famous artists together, but she seems quite content to live in Paradise. It's great fun for me to jingle my keys and see all the animals scampering out to be fed. I have a theory that they're all one family—Picasso is the mother, Dali is the father, and the other three are their kittens. Very recently, a new gray-and-white addition to the artist's colony turned up to be fed, and I named him Rodin, my first sculptor in a bunch of painters at Kittens.

Cats is the name of a feeding station about ten blocks away from my home. There are a lot of bushes at the side of a condominium apartment house, and the cats like the protection the cover gives them. When it snows Cats is a hard place to get to, so Sheilah always drives me there. The cats who hang around there are Tiger Girl, Lion Girl, Panther Girl, Jaguar Girl, Cheetah Girl, Ocelot Girl, Leopard Girl, Cat Girl. Do you get the idea that a theme might be developing here? I don't know what I'll do if a male ever shows up at Cats. I guess I'd have to go to Tiger Boy, etc. Just as at Kittens, the cats here stay hidden in the bushes until I jingle my keys. That sound acts as a dinner bell and out they all run.

RUBY'S PLACE AND SHELTER

About thirteen blocks from where I live is a gas station, which is also a service station where they fix cars and trucks. It's our third stop, and I call it Ruby's Place, after the cat named Ruby. It's a large feeding station with lots of cats; there's Ruby; Diamond Two; Jade; Onyx; Sapphire; Athos, Portos, Aramis, and D'Artagnan; Phochet; Co Co; Grandpa; White Shadow; Stanley; Flip; Monte Cristo; Samurai; Ninja; Kamakazi; Arigato. Even though it's a large group, the cats seem happy enough hanging around together and getting two squares a day. This is the place where Ginny found the two tuxedo kittens, Black and White, hiding under a car with their dead mother.

When we turn up at Ruby's Place, sometimes some of the cats are waiting, sometimes all of them, sometimes none. They like the parked cars and trucks and they feel comfortable and safe hidden underneath the vehicles, hidden from the hostile world until they hear my "dinner bell." Then they just seem to melt into the picture.

Across the street from the Long Beach Animal Shelter is the feeding station I call Shelter. It's a large parking lot for the trucks attached to the Airtite Window factory, where Ginny found the Chairman under all that glass. The feeding area itself is pretty dangerous, because the cats have to cross the street to get to it, and certain drivers think there's no speed limit. I wouldn't have chosen this spot, but the cats like it and hang around here, and we go where the cats are.

The factory has a big Dumpster full of broken glass, and the cats will gather underneath it when it rains or snows. As we approach the feeding station, Max, Skip, and Leonore come running toward Sheilah's car. I put food down for them so they can start eating, then I ring the dinner bell. Before I can get my keys back in my pocket, Nikki; Felix; Marion; Ruth; Herold, Eric, and Halfdan, my three Vikings;

We first called Izzy "Isabella," when we thought that "he" was a "she."

Ferdinand, Izzy's brother, waits for food.

Bobbie (foreground) and Izzy.

Dinnertime.

At the Monroe feeding station.

Suki; Tessa; Vito; and Mama come on the double to eat. We go through a lot of cat food at Shelter.

When it rains hard, the Shelter parking lot, which is low-lying, sometimes gets flooded. The food bowls would just wash away, so I wrap the food in aluminum foil and try to throw it under the Dumpster, where the cats are taking cover. My aim isn't always wonderful, because I have to pitch with my left arm, but most of the time I can put it across the plate (no pun intended).

HarperCollins

This used to be the Market Street feeding station, but after the first book came out, I renamed it after my publisher, HarperCollins. Some of the cats I feed there are named after the wonderful people we worked with on the book—Larry and Jason, our editors; Marshall, who handled our publicity; and HC's Krista, Lucinda, and Allison. Also eating there are Victoria, Blancmange, Blackpearl, Stripes, and Lucy.

HarperCollins is in a residential area, mostly low-income houses. At first, a lot of the people who live there were definitely not in favor of my feeding the cats. They believed that I was just attracting more cats to yowl and mate under their windows. I explained that I was feeding them, trapping them, having them neutered and spayed, getting them immunized against disease, and, wherever possible, finding them homes. A lot of them calmed down and stopped complaining. But I'm sorry to say there are always people who hate cats.

Sometimes with cat-haters, I get really wicked. I can't

help it. One guy really hated cats and wanted me far gone from Market Street. I told him that it was my intention to trap the cats and have them destroyed. When he heard that, a big smile spread over his face.

Two weeks later, we had a really severe windstorm. A tree was blown down right on his house, and I'm almost ashamed to say that it was my turn to smile, but smile I did. It crossed my mind that perhaps this guy had incurred the wrath of God by wanting to kill His little creatures, but then it occurred to me that the smashed house could very well be revenge taken by Bast, the cat-headed goddess from Ancient Egypt.

TREE AND MONROE

Tree is close to my home, but I'm not crazy about it as a place to feed my outdoor cats. First of all, it's on a concrete island in the middle of two-way traffic. Next, there are really no amenities there—no shelter for the cats. The only reason I use it is because the cats themselves chose it, although there aren't many left who are using it. Still, Rufus, J.B., and Black Two deserve two meals a day as much as any of the others. There are several trees on the island, and I used to feed at the center tree, but some knuckleheads who hate cats were claiming that my feeding them was bringing rats to the spot, and they started dumping garbage and broken beer bottles by the cat tree (as though garbage never attracted a rat!), so I moved the feeding station to the last tree.

Monroe is the furthest area from my home, about a mile

Marshall feeding at the glass factory.

away. It's a corner house with a pool, and it has high bushes that the cats like to hide in. There are about eight cats there, including Freyo, Joanie, Ferdy and Izzy, and Bobbie. Phyllis is gone, I'm sorry to say, and I don't expect to see her ever again in this lifetime. There's also another cat who eats at Monroe; I call him Orange. He's a black cat, but he has large orange eyes and he wears an orange collar. That's right. Orange is a freeloader, a cat who has a home and meals but who likes to snack with the others. I asked around about him and learned his real name is Moses.

As soon as we turn the corner, the cats come running from all directions. But there are a lot of dogs in the neighborhood and often they chase the cats away from the food. When she sees this from the car window, Ginny begins to bark angrily. She's so indignant that I don't dare let her out of the car. There's too much traffic. So I get out myself and start barking just like Ginny. I don't actually chase them, but I yell at the dogs to stop. And they run home, which never fails to take me by surprise. Maybe my bark is as authoritative as Ginny's, although I doubt it.

THE LOOKOUTS

In the old days, when ships crossed the oceans under full sail, there was always a lookout posted high up in the rigging, in what they called a crow's nest. It was the lookout's job to sight land, whales, oncoming storms, and other items of maritime interest. Our feeding stations have lookouts, too, designated cats who always spot our coming and alert the others. The items of interest are, of course, the food we're carrying and the presence of Ginny. All the street cats adore Ginny, and she returns their affection.

At Kittens, it's Chagall who's the lookout, sitting there waiting at the top of a tree. (This makes sense, because Chagall the painter often has men and women floating high over his landscapes.) When he sees Sheilah's Camry coming, he runs down the tree and takes up his position at the exact place where I feed. When Picasso, Dali, Rodin, Monet, and Renoir see him, they know it's suppertime and come scampering on the double. Artists are always supposed to be "starving," aren't they? Maybe that's why they always eat so much.

The lookout at Cats is Lion Girl. She's always the hungriest, so she's always the first to see or hear the car, and she makes a feline beeline for the spot where the dishes go down. Right after her comes Tiger Girl, and then the others, one and two at a time.

All-black Allison is the lookout at HarperCollins, and she runs out as soon as she sees the car, followed by Stripes, Blackpearl, and all the others.

At Ruby's Place, Co Co, who is a black-and-white polydactyl, comes from underneath a truck always parked near the feeding station. Within seconds of lookout Co Co's emerging, Athos, Porthos, Aramis, Stanley, and Grandpa are also there.

Van Gogh at the Paradise can tell Sheilah's car from half a block away, but I think that she runs out first as much to see Ginny as to get fed. Of all the outdoor cats, Van Gogh is the most attached to my dog. There are little games they play together, and Van Gogh actually enjoys "riding" Ginny. She jumps on the dog's back and Ginny rides her around.

At the Shelter feeding station, we used to have three lookouts—Beige, Maxine, and Skip, the first ones out to eat. But now that Maxine and Beige have found loving homes, there is only Skip in the crow's nest. When he signals, the other cats are not far behind.

Bobbie and Izzy chow down. Bon appétit!

CHAPTER 6

MORE RESCUES

I CAN'T THINK OF A SINGLE WEEK THAT GOES BY when Ginny doesn't save the life of at least one cat. Now, as I write these words, she has had upwards of two hundred rescues to her credit, and many of them ended in the adoption of another cat or kitten into a deserving home. Ginny has had so many dramatic cat rescues that we are already taking them for granted. We know that she doesn't stop to think about any possible danger for herself—if her special radar detects a cat who needs her help, off she runs to save the day like Mighty Mouse. And I, of course, go chasing after her. Ginny has me well-trained.

But not all of Ginny's rescues can be dramatic. Thank God, because every time she does something foolish, like digging through shards of broken glass or tearing across a busy street to confront an animal we can't see, two or three more hairs on my head turn white. Not every cat Ginny has rescued was saved from broken glass or barbed wire like the Chairman or Roosevelt. A great many saves were pretty tame in comparison, all in a day's work for her. If any other dog had accomplished these rescues, people would make a big fuss over the pup, but for Ginny they were almost ho hum. Yet, each one demonstrates her uncanny ability to locate cats in trouble and her heroic eagerness to get them out of it.

I've been asked how Ginny reacts to seeing a new cat on the street. Can she tell it from one of our regular bunch? Does she whimper? No, she whimpers only in two situations: to tell me that a cat is in trouble or when she wants a particular cat or kitten for herself. Whenever a new cat comes to the dinner table, it's as though we've been feeding it for months. Ginny is very peaceful toward it. Sometimes, although not often, the new cat is apprehensive. In that case, my dog does the Ginny Crawl to ease its mind. If that doesn't work, and the new cat is still nervous, Ginny simply backs off to give it time to adjust.

When the cats are eating, Ginny keeps a firm eye on them. Often, neighborhood dogs will come around to hassle the cats or steal the cat food. As soon as Ginny spots them, she begins to bark. She's about half the size of most of them, but that doesn't faze her. She's there to protect the cats, and she lets the dogs know it. And know it they do, because they don't dare come too close when Ginny is around.

Saving cats is Ginny's mission; she does her job daily and she does it very well, sometimes with bells, whistles, and fireworks, and sometimes quite peacefully.

JOANIE

Take Joanie, for example. One warm, misty night, Ginny and I were out for a walk when she stopped suddenly, pricked up her ears, and stood very still. Her nose twitched, and her tail began to thump. She was staring at a parked truck in a way that clearly said "cat." Then she started to bark and wouldn't quit.

One of the great things about Ginny is that she has a real vocabulary; if you get to know her, you know exactly what she means. If a cat needs her, she barks. If a cat is in real trouble, and Ginny needs a human hand either to help her free it from its prison or to drop her leash so she can get it herself, Ginny will not only bark but whine in a very special way that says, "Help, Philip. You have to help. This is a special circumstance." And of course, Ginny has that very special whimper she reserves when she's determined to have me bring another cat home for her to cuddle. That one just melts my bones; even when I try hard to resist it, I never can.

So when I heard her barking in that familiar way, I listened for the meow that had triggered her, but I couldn't hear anything. Even so, I knew that Ginny had somehow sensed a cat. I got down on my knees and peered under the truck. Sure enough, two round yellow eyes peered back at me. I took my gloves out of my jacket pocket and put them on, then reached under the truck and pulled out the prettiest little gray-and-white kitten.

As soon as Ginny saw her, she stopped barking. Her job

was done. She could trust me. The kitten was now in good hands.

Joanie, as I named her, was very scared. She cringed in my hands and hissed at me in fright. So I set her down on the sidewalk, only a few inches away from Ginny. Ginny snapped into action, immediately licking and grooming the little cat, nibbling at the matted fur. Immediately, the kitten stopped shivering, sat down peacefully, and her eyes closed in bliss. She began to purr; Ginny was such a comfort that she was no longer afraid. Ginny has this remarkable effect on just about every cat we've met on our rounds. They all want to be her favorite, and nudge one another out of the way to be the closest one to her.

After Joanie was neutered and had all her shots, we looked for a home for her, but no luck. So now she's at the Monroe feeding station, where we see her every day. As soon as she catches a glimpse of Ginny, Joanie runs up to be groomed. Ginny puts one paw on her to hold her still while she nibbles the cat's fur. The look of supreme happiness on Joanie's face is the same one she had the night we found her.

IZZY AND FERDINAND

We were out on one of our walks when Ginny ran up to a house and began digging furiously under the deck. It was private property, so I tried to restrain her, but she was in one of those single-minded modes of hers where nothing and nobody can pull her away. By now she was also whimpering that "Cat! Cat! Cat in trouble!" whimper of hers. The little boy who lived there ran in and told his father that a dog was digging up his lawn, and the man came out of his house steaming mad. As soon as he saw us he got madder still.

I tried to explain to him that there was animal life under his deck.

"Probably cats," I told him, "but maybe a raccoon or a possum, which can be very destructive to your property. Ginny always knows what she's doing."

"I don't care! Just get your dog away from my deck!"

But Ginny was in no mood to leave, and she can be very stubborn and persistent. "Just let me take a look," I begged, and I lay down on the ground and peered under the deck, where Ginny was digging. Sure enough. "Kittens."

The fellow lay down next to me and looked under the planking. His eyes opened wide in surprise. Two little cuties had taken up residence under his house.

"Hey, I'm sorry!"

"Don't apologize," I told him. "How could you know?"

We stood up, and I took my position in front of the deck while the house owner jumped up and down on the deck planking. The startled kittens made a run for it, straight at me, and I was able to catch them. They were gray and white, about eight weeks old, and not at all wild.

"Thanks for letting me get them," I said.

"No, thank you for getting them out," he answered, and we were now friendly.

"They're a nice couple of cats. Would you like to give them a home?"

"No. I wish I could, but my boy here is allergic to cats and dogs."

So we shook hands, and I carried them off to the vet's for shots and neutering. They were both male, and Dr. Gelfand said they were between four and five months old. They'd been so undernourished that they hadn't grown. I had named them Isabella and Ferdinand, thinking that they were boy and girl. Since they both turned out to be boys, Isabella soon became Izzy. We left them at the vet's office, hoping they'd find good homes, but nobody adopted them, so they wound up back out on the street with our other outdoor cats, healthy and eating twice a day. I still see them and feed them.

CORY AND DIAMOND

One night while we were out feeding, I could see that Ginny needed a rest room, so I took her out of the car to walk her. As we walked past a house that had a garden, Ginny began to whimper. At first I thought she wanted to use the garden grass to relieve herself on, but I was wrong. Ginny is too much of a lady.

She pulled toward the garden, which featured a wishing well on the lawn. I could see she was heading for the well, which I presumed was deep and filled with water. I keep Ginny on a retractable leash and, when I saw her about to leap into the well, I pulled hard and the leash retracted, stopping her. Then, gently, I pulled her back, but at the same time I was curious, so I went to take a look in the well.

As it turned out, it wasn't a real wishing well after all, just a decorative lawn ornament with very little depth and no water. And inside were hiding two black-and-white kittens about four or five months old. Good old Ginny! She must have remembered the old nursery rhyme, "Ding dong bell, Pussy's in the well."

It was a cold night and I was wearing gloves, so I grabbed up the kittens and ran with them to the car, where I put them into a carrier. Then Sheilah drove us to the All Creatures Veterinary Clinic. Cory and Diamond were at Dr. Gelfand's for only a couple of weeks when they found two good homes and human families to love them.

CASSANDRA

Cassandra was locked in a garage behind an empty house. For about five days, every time we passed that house on one of our walks, Ginny would bark and whimper her cat whimper. I looked through the garage windows, but I couldn't see anything moving. The windows were very dirty. The door was padlocked and it was privately owned property; I had no business snooping around there. Even so, I trusted Ginny's instincts completely. If her barks and whines were telling me that there was a cat in trouble there, then there surely must be one.

On Sunday, we were going past the house again when I saw a crew of workmen there. So I asked them if they would be good enough to open the garage door, and they obliged. You should have seen the looks on their faces when Cassandra came running out. Everybody was surprised except Ginny and me.

We couldn't catch her that day, but the following day I

returned with a cat carrier and some food. I sent Ginny on ahead, knowing that she would have a better chance at drawing out Cassandra than I would. Sure enough, when Cassandra saw Ginny, she came right out of the garage and rubbed against her. While she was with my dog, I opened the carrier door and put some food inside. She walked in without a backward look and settled down to eat. So I had her safe.

From the workmen I pieced together Cassandra's story. She must have been using the garage as shelter, coming and going through a broken window. The guys on the job had no idea there was a cat inside the garage when they replaced the window, and so poor Cassandra got shut in for about a week. She was in pretty good shape except for being emaciated and dehydrated, and as hungry as a pack of wolves. She cleaned up beautifully, a sweet-faced little calico kitten of about six months, with clearly defined markings of orange and black on white fur.

She had no problem finding a home while she was at Dr. Gelfand's office. Cassandra met a married couple who had recently lost their beloved pet cat to cancer. They found Cassandra's fetching ways a mirror image of their cat who'd died; they fell in love with her and took her home.

THE X-FILES

Perhaps this next one wasn't a hair-raising rescue, but it was a very amusing one. One morning Ginny and I were feeding the cats at the Market Street site we now call HarperCollins. Across the street from the feeding station was a large garbage can, and Ginny made for it in a beeline. Before I could stop her, she turned it over. Of course, there was a young cat in it, a cute striped tabby, fairly large, which I scooped up in a carrier. I took him home and isolated him in my bathroom, intending to take him to the veterinarian after the evening feeding. So that night he was to come along feeding with us in a carrier inside the car.

The night of the very same day, we were back at the HarperCollins spot to feed cats, and Ginny ran over to an old chest of drawers which someone had thrown out and began to make a lot of noise. The drawers were out of the piece of furniture, and Ginny kept knocking on it and trying to push her paws down into the remains of the bureau.

"Ginny, quit that!" I ordered. "You're making so much racket that people are going to complain about us and chase us away from here!"

But of course she paid me no attention. She continued scratching and pushing her paws into the chest of drawers. So I reached my bare hand down as a favor to Ginny, and sure enough, there was a cat! She wasn't happy, though, and she hissed at me loudly. I pulled my hand out quickly, because it's the only working hand I have.

Sheilah came running across the street and grabbed up the cat. This was another striped tabby, but with a white shirtfront. We had only the one carrier with us, and this morning's rescue was already in it, but we opened the door and popped the new little cat inside. Then we noticed that the two of them looked exactly alike, except that the one we found in the morning was twice the size of the new little one. They could be sister and brother or, as it turned out, sister and sister, two peas from the same gene-pool pod. They were actually the same age, and could very well have been litter-mates. They'd both been found pretty close together, and both at the same feeding station.

We brought them to Dr. Gelfand. Because they were so alike, except for size, I named them Mulder and Scully, in honor of the two FBI agents from one of my favorite TV shows, "The X-Files." Fox Mulder, played by David Duchovny, is at least a foot taller than his partner, Dana Scully, played by Gillian Anderson. Their Mutt-and-Jeff relationship is one of the funniest visual jokes of the show.

So Mulder and Scully took up residence at the veterinarian's office. A kind of playpen was set up for them, filled with toys and things for them to climb on, and they put on quite a show with their cute kitten antics. We thought they'd be adopted, probably one at a time, but they never lasted long enough to be placed out on the pussycat market. Dr. Gelfand's cousin Dr. Geltman is also a vet in the office, and Dr. Geltman's girlfriend took one look at the pair and whisked them home with her. She even kept their names. I wonder how many cats (and dogs, hamsters, and parakeets) in America (and England, where "The X-Files" is the hottest show) are named Mulder and Scully. Probably thousands. Maybe even tens of thousands.

I have a friend who picked up a stray black-and-white kitten on the day that the Soviets launched their Sputnik rocket, back in the 1950s. She thought that she was being very clever to name her new cat after the spacecraft, but when she took it to the vet to be spayed, the doctor only sighed, "Oh, no! Not another Sputnik!"

Calliope the calico lives with Sheilah; her name means "Pretty Face," and we call her Callie.

Is Callie sleepy or bored? Your call.

WE LOSE ONE

In March of 1996 I trapped a cat named Max from one of our feeding areas and took him to be inoculated and neutered. Dr. Gelfand did the tests and informed me sadly that he had feline leukemia and was terminally ill. We made the sorrowful decision to have Max put to sleep, and his death haunted me for days. I told myself over and over that it was for the best, that he was doomed, that we had spared Max a drawn-out, painful death, that no death was kinder than just to go to sleep and not wake up, that there was nothing veterinary science could do for him, that he might have infected other cats if he'd been left on the street, and that for every cat we lose, we save fifty or more. I know that I take a cat's death too personally, as though it was a failure on my part, and I know, too, that I should learn to let go.

The problem with me is that I see every animal in the world as an individual, with a different personality and nature from all the others. Max had been out on the street all his life, and I'd been feeding him ever since he was a small kitten. I felt as though I had raised him myself, and in a way, I had. Maybe I shouldn't give cats names, but only numbers. Maybe losing "Twenty-three" would be less painful than losing "Max." But I don't think so. A rose is a rose is a rose and a cat is a cat is a cat, no matter what he or she is named. Max was a part of my world and that part is now gone forever.

Everything I told myself about it being okay to let go is true, but I still think of Max's euthanasia as "losing Max." Every time I go feeding the cats and reach Shelter, I see him. It's not only that I *want* to see him, I *do* see him. To me, Max is still hanging around at Shelter and always will be.

Ginny is always on the ball.

CHAPTER 7

GINNY SUPERSTAR

*Y*OU KNOW HOW WHEN you throw a stone into still water it makes ripples that spread out wider and wider until they seem to disappear? And you're never exactly sure of how far those ripples will reach? Well, that's what happened to Ginny and me after our book came out. On that fateful day when Ginny and I met in the animal shelter and fell in love, I could never have guessed in a million years that some day my dog and I would be autographing and "paw-tographing" our own book, that we'd be the subject of newspaper and magazine feature stories and TV talk show interviews.

Most of all, there was no way on earth we could guess that some day Sally Jessy Raphael would tell her national TV audience, "This next story grabbed me by the heartstrings. You see, this hero has saved over fifty lives. Please welcome a real hero, Ginny. Ginny, come on out." And that she'd be talking about my dog.

The ripples are still widening, and I can't imagine where or when they'll ever stop, but my life today is very different from my life before I wrote my book. We've made many new friends and had a little taste of celebrity. Ginny especially is the superstar; the spotlight is on her, and I stand at the edge of it holding on to her leash.

It all began very simply: I was having some litter box problems with one of my cats, so I went to a lecture given by a famous cat therapist, Carole Wilbourn. When she asked her audience how many cats we had, I raised my hand and said eight. Of course, that was in the early days, before the number swelled to nineteen indoor cats and an endless number of outdoor cats. Carole spoke to me privately after the lecture, and I told her about the amazing rescues that Ginny had been making, and about how many of my cats were disabled rejects who would have died without Ginny. Carol was fascinated by the story, and told Phyllis Levy of *Good Housekeeping* magazine. Phyllis, who has since become a wonderful, loyal friend to Ginny, me, and the cats, is a dedicated animal lover. She commissioned an article about Ginny, and the article led to my being contacted by a literary agent, and then to a book. The first stone was thrown into the water and the ripples began.

After the book came out, publicity made those ripples spread even wider. Among the good things that happened were the Mark Walberg talk show, a feature on CNN, the *Newsday* story by Matt Villano, which led to our being invited to speak at schools, "Sally Jessy Raphael," and the

"Leeza" show with Leeza Gibbons. Local news programs picked up the story. We appeared on the Fox Channel 5 news, a New York City station, and on the Channel 55 News, a Long Island station.

Talk show hosts and reporters all tend to want to know the same things: how I found Ginny, how I discovered that she loved cats, what is the source of Ginny's almost magical powers, how could I possibly pay for all those cats we feed, how many cats Ginny has rescued. I soon became almost expert in telling our story. Everybody was fascinated by the Chairman, who was one of Ginny's most recent rescues, and the cameras focused on him. They loved the fact that he is such a friendly and small kitten, and the broken glass and the blood made the telling of his tale perfect material for a show. The Chairman soon became a star in his own right, and a spotlight hog who gave Ginny a real run for the money.

Channel 5 sent reporter Euna Kwon out to Long Beach. She walked Ginny, taking her to the vacant lot where Ginny had made so many rescues and telling the viewer's Ginny's story—from shelter foundling who had been abandoned with her pups to starve to death to beloved pet to full-time rescuer of helpless cats. The crew also took pictures of my indoor cats, showing Madame, the deaf cat; Jackie, the blind one; and Blondie, my poor little AIDS patient—and Ginny looking after them all.

"She's an angel," I said.

"A guardian angel, to cats," answered Euna. "She may look like an ordinary mutt, but this is no ordinary dog. She rescues cats; you might call her the Mother Teresa of the cat world. Ginny can sniff out a cat in need better than a T-bone steak.

Ginny's own sad history may have led to her compassion."

I do believe that this is a big part of it, but not all of it. Ginny's mysterious empathy and compassion for disabled and homeless cats seems to me beyond any simple explanation; there's something very different about that sixth sense of hers that defies definition, but that leads her straight to a cat in trouble. In my opinion, Ginny's wonderful gift can only come from God.

It was probably a combination of the newspaper article and the Fox 5 news feature that brought us to the attention of cable shows, CNN, *Parade*, and Sally Jessy Raphael.

On the "America's Talking" show on cable channel CNBC, Bob Raser said, "America is talking about your dog. That's why we're here." Ginny demonstrated the famous Ginny Crawl, which she uses when she doesn't want to intimidate small children and frightened cats. I took the Chairman out of his carrier and offered him to Ginny, who immediately began to groom him with her teeth.

"See how she cleans him? She nibbles him with her teeth like a mother cat. No other dog does that," I pointed out.

Bob marveled at the scene, especially at how much the kitten loved having his fur chewed by Ginny, and said he'd never heard of a dog like her. He referred to her "mothering instinct," which seems to fascinate everybody who sees Ginny interacting with a cat.

"I've heard of interesting relationships, but this is a three-way going strong," Bob said. "There's you, a man with his heart in the right place, who rescued this little dog Ginny, and Ginny likes cats."

Dr. Jonathan Greenfield of the cable TV show "The

Family Pet" introduced Ginny as "a rather unusual dog who finds injured cats. Ginny, who actually came from the shelter herself, has a strange knack for finding cats." Then, holding the Chairman on his lap and stroking the kitten's ears, Dr. Greenfield told Ginny's story to his viewers. "They're like mother and daughter here," he told his viewers, overlooking the fact that the Chairman is a male.

Like everybody else, the host of "The Family Pet" asked familiar questions.

"If you're feeding eighty cats out there it must cost you a fortune." It does. At least $800 a month for food, and sometimes as much as $1,000 a month on vet bills.

"Ginny's strange way of finding disabled cats. Any ideas about how she does it?" She has a kind of sixth sense.

"When you're feeding the feral cats, aren't you a little nervous about increasing the feral cat population?" No, because I capture them one by one and take them in to be neutered.

"You're like a Pied Piper of cats, aren't you?" No, it's Ginny they consider the Pied Piper of Long Beach, not me.

"Has this changed your life at all?" That's probably the easiest question to answer. It's given me a new purpose in life. All these stray animals need help, they need to live.

CNN sent Mary Anne McRae from the feature "A Different Story" out to Long Beach to come feeding with us. She called us "a kind of Meals on Wheels for cats," and noted that "all these cats are healthy now; even the wild ones look sleek and fed." When we pulled up to one of our feeding stations, some of the cats ignored Sheilah's car and went instead up to the CNN mobile TV van. They might have been confused by the bright lights on the van, but I suspect that the cats might simply have wanted their fifteen minutes of fame on TV. Mary Anne asked me if people say or think I'm crazy and I admitted that some people do.

"Are you crazy?" she asked.

"No." I shook my head. "I'm really sane. I received a new lease on life, and I'm just passing it along to the cats."

"Ginny's exploits sound like one of those high drama search-and-rescue shows you see on television."

CNN also interviewed our veterinarian, Dr. Lewis Gelfand, in the office of his practice. He said that he had never seen or even heard of a dog who did the things that Ginny does. "This dog is very different from any other dog out there. I have two dogs, and they might chase cats, but they would never, never rescue them. This behavior puts Ginny in a class by herself."

Mary Anne then explained how it was Ginny who had given me my new lease on life and all the while the camera was on Ginny, sitting quietly and smiling as she watched her indoor cats happily stuffing their faces.

"Eyewitness News," on New York's Channel 7, came along with us as we fed our cats at the Tree. Their reporter called Ginny "not the most beautiful animal in the world, but Ginny is not your ordinary dog." Why do people keep saying that? To me, Ginny Gonzalez *is* the most beautiful dog in the world. Certainly, anybody looking into that winsome face will never forget those huge bright eyes with their intelligent expression. And Ginny's sweet smile knocks on the door of your heart.

"So far," the voice-over continued, "Ginny has rescued about two hundred cats. Ginny loves them all as though they were her own, and I guess they are."

News 55, a Long Island station, sent Sara Muller, a young woman with an obvious love for animals, to meet with Sheilah, Ginny, and me. She and Ginny got along like a house afire, and Ginny seemed never to want to stop kissing Sara.

"It sounds hard to believe, but this small dog has touched two hundred lives, both big and small," said Sara. "Her name is Ginny, and she's the Pied Piper of sick and disabled cats. Sheilah says she's never rescued a healthy cat, but thanks to the help of Ginny, Sheilah, and Philip—and their veterinarian—they've all been nursed back to health."

Sheilah pointed out, "She has this sixth sense of radar, and can pick out sick and injured animals from bushes, from buildings, from trailers, brown paper bags, from empty boxes." Not to mention cartons of broken glass, garbage cans, air-conditioning ducts, eight-inch pipes, and a lot of other unlikely places.

"At four A.M. and then again at dusk, Sheilah and Philip put Ginny in the car for a feeding tour," Sara explained. Film showed us arriving at a feeding station, and the cats running toward us, eager to be fed. Then we went back home to finish the story.

The camera picked up some of Ginny's own special babies—Topsy rolling around the floor; Blondie, my FIV cat, peering out of her cage; Betty Boop hopping around like a rabbit; and Madame, sitting in all her dignity and beauty, in her silent world. It was one of the best pieces done on us.

Every article and every news or talk show made us more "famous." Each time Ginny and I went public there was a surge of recognition, with people actually stopping their cars and getting out to pet Ginny when they saw me walking her. But with Sally Jessy Raphael's show came nationwide celebrity.

The first coast-to-coast syndicated television talk show we guested on was "Sally Jessy Raphael." Her topic was "You're My Hero!" She had invited a group of guests who had performed selfless heroic deeds, including my Ginny. Among the unsung heroes were a 911 operator who saved a choking baby over the phone, a police officer who rescued a woman from drowning, and a mother who saved her daughter and her daughter's friends from carbon monoxide poisoning. They all spoke about their rescues, but Ginny was the only animal on the show. All the unsung heroes were to receive medals from Sally herself.

We came on last, closing the show. I was sitting on the stage and Ginny was in the wings, waiting for her big entrance. We'd actually been in the studio for almost five hours for our few seconds of fame, but it was worth it. When Sally said, "Come on out," Ginny emerged from behind the curtain and began to come toward me. As soon as the audience saw her, they burst into applause and cheers.

The unexpected noise stopped Ginny in her tracks. She'd never heard anything like it before, and it scared her. So she turned around and started to head backstage again. This time the audience began to laugh, and a lot of them murmured, "Aaaawwww," the way people do when they're touched. Sally called to her, I called to her, but Ginny was having a sudden attack of stage fright. With a little more of my coaxing, Ginny came out again. Once she was actually on stage she behaved like a superstar. She immediately began to say hello to the people sitting in the front row, who were holding their hands out to pet her and waggling their fingers for her to sniff and lick.

"She *loves* cats?"

"She loves cats."

"She *rescues* cats?"

"She rescues cats."

"She really saved fifty lives?" asked Sally.

"More than fifty."

Sally asked about her breed, and I gave her Ginny's noble lineage—part schnauzer, part Siberian husky, part heaven only knows what. I told the audience that Ginny had come from a humane society shelter.

"We're very pleased to meet you. A lot of our friends come from the humane society," Sally said, rubbing Ginny's ears.

Then I described how Ginny had rescued an abandoned litter of five really small kittens by finding them at the bottom of a large pipe in a construction site. Meanwhile, Spot, one of the kittens from that litter, was waiting nervously backstage for his own appearance. When Sally finally summoned Spot onstage, he came out in the arms of our HarperCollins editor Jason Kaufman, and boy, was he scared! Spot, that is, not Jason. The laughter and applause only freaked him out even more. He struggled and squirmed until I got him into my own arms, where he half-settled but began to howl.

Spot howled while Sally hung a hero's medal around Ginny's neck. He howled while Ginny and Sally exchanged kisses. He howled while Sally made her closing remarks to the audience. Only I knew what Spot was trying to say. It was, "Get me out of here! Take me home! Hoooommme!"

The most recent TV talk show we did—or rather *I* did—

Spot lives with Sheilah, but Ginny visits daily.

was the Leeza Gibbons program, which was doing a theme of animal heroes with unusual stories. They invited us both, of course, but the program is taped in Los Angeles, and the program's representative informed me that Ginny would have to travel in a box in the baggage compartment.

Thanks, but no thanks, I said. Never mind the stories about one airline losing a pet cat in its fuselage for more than a week, and the same airline later losing a dog. I remember seeing a segment on one of the magazine shows about the terrible things that can happen to animals when they ride in the baggage hold of an aircraft. Not *my* Ginny. I would never allow her to travel by air except by my side.

The "Leeza" show didn't want to pay for a seat for Ginny. However, they told me that I could appear without her, and I accepted, although looking back I'm not so sure that was such a good idea. Ginny without me probably makes a better impression than I do without her. We both have big brown eyes, but she has that wagging tail and a smile that melts hearts. And Ginny isn't shy, but I am, so she's a lot more telegenic and is not reluctant to open her mouth.

I left from Kennedy on a Tuesday morning, and the flight took all of six and a half hours. There was a lot of turbulence. When I arrived at LAX (Los Angeles Airport) there was a car waiting for me, and it took me right to the studio. I was put in a trailer on the lot to dress; then I waited in Studio 53 for the taping to begin.

There I met the other guests and their dogs, who were going to be on the show. They were an impressive bunch. There were two K-9 police dogs, one a Belgian shepherd and the other a German shepherd, who chased down, caught, and held a suspect even after he stabbed them both. There were two greyhounds who had found homes after their racing days were over. An organization helps these poor exploited dogs get good homes for the balance of their days, after they've grown too old or too weak for racing. One of the dogs, Natasha, was so unused to being in a home that she raced right into the swimming pool and nearly drowned.

A cute little Chihuahua named Chilly Willie was paralyzed in its back legs, and a tiny wheelchair had been made for its hindquarters, no more than a foot high, allowing it to roll around. I was reminded of my own precious Topsy, the brain-damaged cat whom Ginny rescued, who can't stand up or walk. Topsy, too, rolls around on the floor to get to where she wants to go. Animals can be so gallant.

A pit bull whose name is Weela saved about thirty people from drowning. A dam broke, and Weela headed off the people who were trying to cross the river. She ran in front of them, barking very loudly, and turned them away, just as a sheepdog does with sheep. If they hadn't run in the other direction, those men, women, and children would have been caught up in the rushing dam rivers and surely died. So Weela was a real hero.

Robert O'Barry, the trainer of the famous dolphin Flipper, was on the show, too. Mr. O'Barry is now against training dolphins in captivity; he thinks they should all swim free. Flipper died in his arms. His was a very moving story.

I did the best I knew how, telling the audience and Leeza about how Ginny and I found each other and how she surprises the world by rescuing cats. But I could tell that a number of people were really disappointed not to have Ginny there. Leeza was, too. She asked for an autographed book, but I hadn't brought one with me, so I promised to send her one with Ginny's paw print. It was really Ginny's autograph Leeza wanted, not mine. It doesn't take a genius to figure out who is the true superstar in the team of Philip and Ginny Gonzalez.

So far, Ginny's story has appeared in print in *Good Housekeeping, Newsday, Parade,* and the *Enquirer.* With each exposure—print or television—she and I have become more familiar to strangers, not only in Long Beach but around the country. I'm always surprised when people come up to me after a TV show and tell me they've read our book or seen us in *Parade* or somewhere else. It takes some getting used to, being recognized. Ginny, of course, thrives on it. The more hands reaching out to pet her, the better she likes it.

One of the events that was most satisfying was the autographing party and discussion at the big Barnes & Noble bookstore at Rockefeller Center. March is Pet Responsibility Month. Every Thursday and Friday during March 1996, Barnes & Noble held seminars, open to the public and free of charge, with guests of honor who were authors of well-known pet-related books. The idea behind the seminars was to help pet owners and animal lovers become more aware of the latest trends in animal health care, training techniques, preventive care, and communicating with pets. The series also promoted the Humane Society of New York, its services, and the vital role it plays in the New York community.

Ginny and I were invited to be the authors at the first seminar, March 7, and to sign our book for their customers. It was flattering to be first, especially when you consider the great lineup Barnes & Noble had arranged for the month, including, among others, Dr. Michael Rubinstein, the clinic director of the Humane Society of New York; Dr. Allen Shoen, the author of *Love, Miracles and Animal Healing*; and Carole Wilbourn, the well-known cat therapist who had started me on the way to writing a book in the first place. Carole is the author of *Cat Talk* and other books.

March 7 turned out to be a cold, wet, and windy day, complete with sleet in the face and ice underfoot. I was scared stiff that nobody would turn up for us in such bad weather. HarperCollins (the publisher, not the feeding station) sent a car for us, but the roads from Long Beach into the city were bumper-to-bumper, and we were going to be at least a few minutes late. I was nervous all the way in, torn between anxiety over not being on time and fear that I'd be facing empty chairs.

When we pulled up in front of Barnes & Noble on Forty-eighth Street and Fifth Avenue, I took the Chairman and handed Ginny's leash to Sheilah, so Ginny could have a walk before showtime. I carried the Chairman downstairs to the lower selling level, where a large section of the bookstore had been set aside for a kind of auditorium, with a TV/VCR and at least sixty chairs set up. And every one of those chairs was filled; there was standing room only.

Our friend Phyllis Levy was there, and she took the Chairman from me and held him in her arms, where he was quite content. Later, he was sort of passed around the audience, since everybody wanted to stroke and pet him.

Bill Edwards, the community relations coordinator for the Barnes & Noble chain, was already addressing the audience when I came down the stairs with the Chairman, and he introduced me.

"I'm sorry Ginny's not here, she's being walked," I told the crowd.

"She's here!" they yelled back, and, sure enough, there was the Love Mop already circulating, kissing hands, licking faces, saying hello to everybody, her tail going like a motor.

The crowd was very well-dressed; probably most of them worked in the Rockefeller Center area and were here on their lunch hour. Most of them were women, but there must have been about fifteen men in the audience. Everybody there had something important in common: They were all animal lovers. I started off by telling them about my accident, and how finding Ginny and helping her in her miraculous rescues snapped me out of my depression and changed my direction to an entirely new path. Then I explained how I was never into cats before, and would never have believed that I'd end up living with nineteen cats, feeding eighty, and loving every minute of it.

Then I played the VCR tape I'd brought with me showing the CNN interview and some footage that Sheilah and I had taken of our own cats, indoor and outdoor. This gave the audience some idea of what I'd been talking about, and of how Ginny interacts with the cats, mothering them and even bossing them around. She's a loving parent, but a good disciplinarian.

After I finished my story and showed my tape, there was a lively question and answer period, and the grown-ups asked much the same kind of questions that the children did in the schools we visited. How old is Ginny? Seven years old on April 1, 1996. How many cats do I have? Was my arm getting better? Only a little better; it's probably never going to perform any better than twenty percent of its capacity. How many cats do I feed and how do I pay for the food? As many cats as I can, usually about eighty. And I pay for it the best way I can, out of my book earnings and my disability check. Did Ginny ever have any pups? Yes, she did. Did her pups like cats? Only for lunch. How do you explain Ginny's special radar of the heart? It can't explain it at all, I had to admit. It's one of heaven's great mysteries. I can only witness it and marvel.

There were several offers to adopt the Chairman, and I kicked myself that I hadn't brought along one or two of the cats we had waiting at All Creatures for adoption. Of course, the Chairman is pretty special; not only was he the subject of one of Ginny's most dramatic rescues, but he's a ham through and through. Like Ginny herself, little Mr. Personality can never have too much affection, and he'll go to anybody who holds a hand out.

It was getting late, and the audience had to go back to work, so Ginny and I started signing books as fast as we could, me with a pen and Ginny with a stamp pad and her front paw. I signed more than a hundred books, and people were buying them right and left, lining up for the autographs. I'll tell you that it gave me a whole new kind of thrill, to know that people out there were willing to pay to read our story. It made me feel like a real author.

One public appearance I made with Ginny was unexpected and very last-minute. On October 5, 1996, the Long Island Cat Fanciers were scheduled to give Dr. Lewis Gelfand, owner of the All Creatures veterinary practice, an Honorary Membership Award for "his dedicated service to educating the public in taking care of cats." Since Dr. Gelfand is our great friend and great vet, Sheilah, Ginny, and I naturally were there in our Sunday best to see him honored.

Well, Dr. Gelfand never showed up. There was some consternation, which really escalated into panic when it was discovered that he'd never been invited! Everybody thought that somebody else in the association had sent him his invitation and informed him that he was to be a guest of honor.

So we were there and he was not. What to do? The Fanciers asked me and Sheilah to fill in and talk about Ginny and her miraculous rescues of injured cats and kittens, and by now I was pretty used to telling her story. I went over for the umpteenth time the strange and wonderful facts of Ginny's life as a guardian angel; then Sheilah told the audience about some of my dog's more recent rescues—the Chairman, of course, because that's always a big crowd pleaser; Black and White; and Mulder and Scully.

It was great to talk to people who were all cat lovers, and who drank in every word. While Sheilah and I were talking, Ginny was doing her number, making the rounds of the audience, kissing everybody she could get her muzzle on.

After the evening was over, Sheilah helped a woman Fancier trap a pregnant feral cat and get her to the vet's. All in all, it was a much more strenuous evening than any of the three of us had expected when we turned up to be spectators.

I'm writing this in March of 1996, and come next October Ginny will be receiving the Humanitarian Award of the Long Island Cat Fanciers Association. It's the first time they're giving one, and certainly the first time that they're giving it to an animal (Ginny puts a spin on the "human" in humanitarian). We're told that it will be a plaque recognizing Ginny's efforts,

At the Barnes & Noble book signing. Our editor, Jason Kaufman, stamps Ginny's "Paw-tograph" for a fan.

although she's a member of a different species, in doing more for cats than most people ever do. The award will be given in connection with a Pet Expo the association is holding, including a pet show for housecats and pedigreed cats.

I asked Art Ackerman, founder and president of the Long Island Cat Fanciers, if my name was going to be on the plaque along with Ginny's. All he said was, "Maybe. We'll see."

I don't really care much about being famous, because I would go on feeding hungry cats and helping my Ginny with her rescues even if nobody else patted me on the back for it. But I have to confess that I do get a kick out of the attention and praise; it took me by surprise, but it warms my heart to know that so many people are interested in saving homeless animals, and so many people want to hear Ginny's and my story. Like Ginny, I enjoy being stroked, too. We've made more new friends than I could ever have imagined.

But as for Ginny, she's just completely happy all day long. Much more than me, she thrives on attention. She gets praise and approval and incredible amounts of affection from children, grown-ups, and cats. She spends all day with her beloved people, me and Sheilah, and spends much of her time mothering her beloved cats. She is constantly on the lookout for new cats and kittens to help. Her radar's antennae are always extended to catch a homeless feline in trouble. Throw in an occasional piece of baked salmon, and Ginny Gonzalez is living the kind of life a dog only dreams of.

As CNN's Mary Anne McRae said of Ginny on "A Different Story," "Fame hasn't gone to her head. Saving cats, it seems, is her number one priority."

Through the screen door, a peaceful scene with Madame and Ginny.

CHAPTER 8

Ginny's Special Friends

CALL ME NAIVE AND I WON'T DENY IT. When I signed up to do a book about Ginny, I was so excited that I didn't look much beyond finishing it and seeing it in print. The hope that strangers would read about my miraculous pup and her angelic rescues was enough for me. I never considered for a minute that we would become sort of famous, or that there would ever be such an outpouring of love toward us from people we'd never even met.

The Dog Who Rescues Cats was published in October, in

time for Christmas 1995. As we hoped, it made a welcome Christmas present for animal lovers. Between mid-December and the New Year, letters began to pour in to HarperCollins' offices, letters from readers who had been moved by the stories of the wretched cats Ginny, Sheilah, and I had rescued. A number of them told us they'd received the book for Christmas, and a surprising number of them contained checks, most of them small checks from $5 to $25, but there were also gifts of $100 and even $250. They soon added up.

I was stunned. I swear to you, I was completely blown away by the letters and the checks. This was something I never expected and certainly never hoped for. It was like making a whole new group of friends, friends who already knew and loved Ginny. For a short time, I didn't know what I should do about the money. I hadn't written the book to solicit contributions. It never occurred to me that people might send me, a total stranger, money to be put toward our rescue work.

Did I have a right to keep the money? Should I send it back? Embarrassed, I agonized over it for several days, and then it occurred to me that sending the money back would not only be sort of insulting, a rejection, but it would rob our new friends of the opportunity they were asking for: to help Ginny in caring for homeless cats. So the money was accepted gratefully and immediately paid out. Half of it went to the cat food wholesaler, and the other half to Dr. Gelfand, to chip away at the national debt—our eternally outstanding bill at the All Creatures Veterinary Clinic. One hundred cents of every dollar sent to me was spent on

Ginny's outdoor cats and her new rescues, either for food or for medical care.

I never realized that so many good people would open their hearts and their pockets to Ginny and me. It overwhelmed me to think of how many lives we had touched by Ginny's unique story. I want to share just a few of the letters we received, because so many writers told us about their own animals, some of whom were rescue stories, such as Sue Bronstrup, who wrote from Ohio:

> My husband and I have ourselves given a home to many cats (either strays or from our shelter) over the years, and we currently have eight and a little dog who is almost twelve years old. Our dog Penny was found by us when she was very young, near starvation, unable to move from the spot in the middle of the lane of traffic where she had— incredibly—been placed on a towel, apparently so that she would be run over! She was covered with mange, but she made a complete recovery and is now very happy with her cat and human family!
>
> My husband Jim and I feel very strongly about animal rights, so we applaud your selfless compassion and the humility that allows you to recognize Ginny's special nature! I honestly feel that there are three angels—Ginny, you, and Sheilah! Thank you for sharing the blessing of Ginny with all of us.

Sue also enclosed a portrait of Ginny, taken from the cover photo, which she'd done in pastels with a mauve mat and a silver frame around it. Sue's picture now hangs in my home, in a place of honor in the living room where I can see it while I'm on the phone and whenever I walk into my kitchen to feed my indoor cats.

There are many more angels in the world than three, and two of them are Sue and Jim Bronstrup, who didn't hesitate to stop and pick up a mangy abandoned pup, and who had enough love in their hearts to recognize a precious soul when they saw one.

Lisa and Troy Hardison wrote from Florida:

> Animal neglect and cruelty is something we detest and we wish there were many more people like you. If we had the means and the time, we'd have so many animals! We have a few now . . . our own angel, Smokey (she's three!), our *beautiful* black lab. We love her. She goes to work with us every day! We have one cat (saved from someone who wanted to be "rid" of him), two nondomestic rabbits (meaning they aren't the cuddly pettable kind), again saved. Then we have fish.
>
> We've talked about your book to a lot of people. You should get it into older folks' homes *and* schools. It's wonderful!

On the top border of the letter Marge Othrow sent me was a wonderful little portrait, done in four colors, of "angel" Ginny, complete with wings and a halo. Marge, too, had copied Ginny's photo off the book jacket, turning it into a small work of art that I treasure. Wrote Marge:

> A copy of *The Dog Who Rescues Cats* was given me as a Christmas gift, and I finished reading it yesterday. What a

wonderful creature Ginny is, and how lucky you both are to have found each other, and what a perfect life you are leading! Bless you all (Sheilah, too!).

As I said, I finished reading your book yesterday, and some time during the night I woke from a very happy dream. I'd been in Grand Central Station, which was filled to bursting with *mobs* of people, and I was being rushed around to meet many of them, perhaps twenty-five or thirty of them. I was so happy to meet them; they—no, we all— were just so ebullient! I have never been in a crowd of such ecstatically happy people. But it wasn't until I woke up that I interpreted the sensation that I had been *tugged* toward all those meetings—and I realized that I had been on the hand- holding end of a leash, and that the spirit—the enthusiastic personality on the other end of the leash—was the one who was racing around "introducing me" to all these friends.

Perhaps I will never meet Ginny "in the fur"—but it pleases me to think I had an adventure with her in spirit and am flattered that she was so happy to introduce me to so many of her friends!

From Naomi Utensky:

I'm sure that you will put this donation to good use in your cat rescue work. I was moved to tears (many tears) by the article in *Newsday*. You and Ginny and Sheilah are an amazing team—I just hope that the recent publicity brings a lot of checks your way so you can continue doing this incredible animal rescue work!

From the bottom of my heart, I thank you—

And she signed her name, adding "and Josie (dog), Emma (cat), Vilda (cat) & Charlotte (cat)."

Marjorie Wittner sent us a generous contribution with the sweetest note:

> I had the enormous pleasure of seeing you on the news Friday night. I was so touched, and I wanted to thank you and your precious dog very, very much for your tremendous generosity and kindness to the blessed strays. You certainly are a modern St. Francis, and I know only too well, because I have also lived my life for the animals, the sorrow and the joy in your rescuing work.
>
> You and your dog are simply wonderful, and I wish you and all your fur-face friends the best of everything in the days and years to come. No one deserves it more.

Whew! A modern St. Francis? Who, me? No, I don't dare make a claim like that for myself, although Ginny might be described as a canine St. Francis. I'm having too much fun doing what I'm doing to be called saintly. But thank you for the thought.

Ileana "Lili" Negron took us totally by surprise.

> I will send you $10 every two weeks, which is what I can afford. Whenever I can send more, I will. I have two cats of my own. They are Mishue and Spanky. I also have four stray cats I feed outside every day.
>
> I feel what you're doing is beautiful. If we had more people like you, the world would be heaven. I pray for you and Ginny. May God bless you both!

A great many of the letter writers expressed a strong spiritual side, saying that they were including us in their prayers, sending us blessings from God, which to me is the greatest gift of all, more valuable by far than money.

Karen Soullier sent us a check and her blessings:

> I saw you and Ginny on "Headline News," and I was deeply touched. You are a very compassionate human being and Ginny—well, she is truly one of a kind.
>
> I have enclosed a check to help you in your efforts. You and Ginny will be in my prayers and I will continue to help out as often as I can. God bless you and Ginny.

Sheila Edwards, from the Bay Area in California, wrote:

> I got your book *The Dog Who Rescues Cats* and read it through in one day. It is too wonderful to put down. I am rereading it immediately.
>
> Your story (and Ginny's) is a true miracle. I have felt renewed by reading your book. When circumstances or incidents stop you long enough to center your spiritual self, then you must acknowledge those who are responsible for that renewal. I must take the time to thank you for what you have given to me through your service to the homeless and helpless cats in Long Island.
>
> I have been drawn into a love and communion with cats, just as you have, through my relationship with my two adopted mongrel cats. I named them Mickey and Minnie. Mickey was killed by raccoons when he was three. It was a terrible loss for me because he was so loving. Minnie is

almost eight now. She is great company and I would have many more cats if I had my own home (we share a house with a friend of ours). I also carry dog and cat food in my car and feed animals when I find them in need, just as you do.

Rebecca Beard wrote all the way from Alaska:

I have read *The Dog Who Rescues Cats* a number of times over the past few weeks. While I love cats, I'm allergic to them, so I restrict myself to two dogs (whom I also love). I got YoYo, a sheltie/dachshund/Pekingese mix, from the SPCA almost eight years ago. She was a six-month-old puppy who had been living as a stray before some good Samaritan picked her up and turned her into the SPCA. Munchkin is a Scottish terrier who was turned over to Friends of Pets, another local rescue organization, when she appeared to need thousands of dollars of medical care. They had a family and couldn't afford a big-ticket item pet. Actually, all she needed was a better vet, a thyroid test, and spaying. She now is healthy (if overweight) and happy.

Becky signed off with a P.S. "YoYo and Munchkin send their regards to Ginny, but they *don't* understand her affection for cats."

From Vermont, Deborah and John Martin and their four pets sent us special holiday greetings. Deborah wrote:

My husband and I read your story aloud for several evenings. It was difficult at times to continue because we were overwhelmed with the love and generosity shown by

Ginny making short work of a Quarter Pounder; for the first time, she ate the bun, too.

both of you under so many difficult and unusual circum-
stances.

We have a Border Collie. Her name is Daisy. We got
her as an eight-week-old puppy from the local Humane
Society about three years ago. She's smart, funny, loving,
and a great watchdog. Our three cats, Pepper, Angel
Buttons, and Misty, were each rescued over a period of five
years. They're each very special in their own unique way.

There were so many letters (and they're still coming in)
that I'd love to include them all, but they'd make a book in
themselves.

My coauthor, Leonore Fleischer, has five cats. Christofur
and Jennifur were adopted from an underprivileged home
and it took a very long time to get them to use their litter
box (Jennifur still makes an occasional mistake). Honey
came as a birthday present from an upstate New York apple
farm, and Sam was picked up on the street in Los Angeles
by a friend of Leonore's. Sam was less than two weeks old,
and had been thrown away like yesterday's newspaper. He
had to be eye dropper–fed around the clock for weeks
before it was certain he would live, but he's now thirteen
years old and going strong. Sam eats like a lumberjack, but
still has that starving, waiflike look that makes everybody
who sees him take pity on him. What a phony!

But Mitzi, a small tuxedo, is the darling of Leonore's
heart, and there is a funny story about how she was adopted.
I'll ask her to tell it.

"One Friday afternoon at the end of June, I visited Bide-
A-Wee animal shelter in New York City, looking for a kitten

for my son, who was suffering from adolescent depression and had little interest in anything. I knew exactly what sort of kitten would cheer him up—no more than eight or nine weeks old, male, small enough to fit in the palm of my hand, and with fluffy red-gold fur. My son's favorite kind, a marmalade like Orlando, the famous literary cat. We had all the Orlando books, and my boy had a cat exactly like that when he was very small, before his allergies developed and Gorman had to find a new home. He hadn't had a cat since then, or any other pet to bond with. He missed Gorman for a very long time.

"Half an hour later I left the Bide-A-Wee with a yowling, rattling cardboard box containing an adolescent female with black-and-white fur, irregular markings, a long nose, huge bat ears, and a squalling voice. She was hideous and I didn't like her, but there were no tiny red kittens for adoption that day, and this homely one insisted on coming home with me, mewing and scampering around her cage, virtually dancing and singing with a straw hat and cane. Resigned, I thought, Oh, well, at least she's healthy and lively, but I *do* prefer a cat with a short nose and small ears!

"The only thing my son treasured was a small houseplant he was growing on his windowsill, a straggly seedling which probably would not have survived the soot and dirt of Manhattan. I brought the cat box inside, opened it, and suddenly this long-legged yowler dashed through the apartment without looking to the right or the left, into my son's bedroom and—with one single decisive chomp—destroyed his precious plant forever!

"My son uttered a howl of rage! He detested the cat on

sight, and threatened to throw her out the window. Exhausted, I lied that Bide-A-Wee closes for the weekend, and I swore I would take her back on Monday. By Monday morning, two totally infatuated humans were following this homely, amusing kitten all around the apartment, not letting her out of their sight, completely captivated by her cleverness, her bright, affectionate personality, her many self-taught playful tricks.

"That was seventeen years ago; my son grew up, married, and has a son of his own, but the black-and-white cat is still the pampered darling of my heart, the world's most loving and intelligent cat. She was even clever enough to grow up around her nose and ears, which are now satisfyingly short. Her squalling voice has deepened into a golden contralto. She is beautiful, inside and out.

"For weeks I couldn't think of the right name for the new little cat—I who in the past had come up with such elegant feline monikers as Felicia Fleischer, Fletcher Fleischer, DeHavilland Pussmoth, Cattermole. One evening *South Pacific* was on television. And there was Mitzi Gaynor, not pretty but healthy and lively, singing and dancing her funny little heart out, and a star. I looked down at the creature purring in my lap. What a resemblance!

"'Mitzi?'

"'Mmmrrrr?'

"And that was that. I didn't realize until later that 'mitzvah' is the Hebrew word for 'blessing,' but now I think that 'Mitzi' must be short for 'mitzvah.' It's very appropriate, because she has so blessed my life. I love all my cats dearly, but Mitzi has my heart firmly and forever in her little paws."

After Mitzi and Leonore lived together for a few years, it began to gnaw at Leonore that she'd cheated Bide-A-Wee out of a million-dollar pet for a paltry twenty dollars, which is what she paid them when she adopted the Mit. So she began to make annual contributions to various good animal causes; every year on Mitzi's birthday (Valentine's Day) she would donate ten dollars for every year of her cat's life, plus ten dollars "to grow on." In 1994, after Mitzi turned sweet sixteen, she gave Ginny a check for $170 for cat food; in 1995, it was $180. Leonore says that she hopes to be donating $1,000 in the far, far distant future, when Mitzi turns ninety-nine.

Maxine Beige is another very special friend who has been incredibly good to us. The "mommy" of eight cats and a dog, she came to us originally through the *Newsday* article, and she knocked us out with a wonderful letter and an extremely large check! At first I thought someone was playing a joke on me. We couldn't find her because Maxine hadn't put a return address on her letter and there was none on her check. So we deposited the check and, to our great surprise, it cleared.

Eventually Sheilah was able to track Ms. Beige down through her bank, so we were able to write her and give our thanks. In reply, she sent us another check for the same amount, as a Christmas present! We named Maxine and Beige after her, and the money she sent us helped us find homes for those two. We finally met our benefactor face-to-face at the book signing at Barnes & Noble, when Sheilah and Maxine hugged each other tightly.

Maxine came up to the table where I was signing books.

"Do you know me?" she asked. Of course I didn't. I had some mental picture of her as a much older woman, one who had a lot of free time, a lot of money, and a very good heart. Here in front of me was a much younger, more vital and busy person than I expected. That'll teach me to make judgments without enough information.

Maxine Beige has recently sent us another equally generous donation. Every penny is spent on the cats, of course, just as she expects. She writes lovingly to Ginny:

> I hope your Mom & Dad [Maxine means Sheilah and Philip] sell a million copies of this book and HarperCollins employees have to work overtime producing this book to meet the consumer demand.
>
> I received mail from Maxine and Beige Gonzalez. I am truly and sincerely honored that your Mom and Dad named a kitten after my given name and an older cat after my family name. Give Maxine Gonzalez and Beige Gonzalez each a hug from me, as well as the others . . . Now that a kitten and cat have my name and I am your "aunt" I will have to call Mommy and Daddy sometime in 1996 and pay them and you and Maxine and Beige and all the rest a visit.

When she does visit, we'll all give her a hero's welcome. To us, Maxine wrote:

> Philip, I agree completely with your views. You are taking care of homeless cats by feeding them and at the same time seeing that their population does not increase and

cause more animal suffering by being responsible and spaying and neutering as many as possible.

May God bless you, Philip, Sheilah, and Ginny for this and everything you are doing . . . and all the animal lives you are saving.

I want to tell all of Ginny's and my good friends that God has indeed blessed me and blessed Sheilah. First, with Ginny, with her affection, and the loving warmth of her company. Then, with the wonderful work she does that she allows Sheilah and me to help her with. And, not least by any means, with this outpouring of friendship and generosity that has made me feel so much better about human nature. When I first began rescuing cats, I witnessed the terrible cruelties that helpless animals are too often subjected to. As a result, I formed a pretty jaundiced opinion of the human race.

But the letters of encouragement and the heartfelt donations that keep pouring in to Ginny and me have made me revise my opinion of human nature. For every cruel person out there, there must be 100 . . . 1,000 men and women and boys and girls with loving, caring hearts. I always did think that the Lord would provide, and how He has!

Ginny at the beach, combining two of her favorite games: digging holes and playing Frisbee. She's burying the Frisbee.

CHAPTER 9

Unique Ginny

GINNY'S STRANGE AFFECTION for cats seems to puzzle everyone who hears about it. A number of readers have written to ask me to explain it, while others have written to give me their own answer to that question. Quite a few explanations have been offered, and a number of interesting theories put forward. It's true that cats and dogs are not necessarily natural enemies—many families have cats and dogs together as pets, and they get along perfectly well, even lovingly. I personally know of one woman who keeps two cats and two dogs and each of the dogs has "her own" cat—she grooms it (although with her tongue, not like Ginny, who uses her teeth) and sleeps with one paw wrapped around it. The two cats thrive on the closeness and love their canine "mothers."

The dogs I owned years ago, Husky and, later, Montoose, both really hated cats. They ran after cats every time they saw them, and would have torn them to pieces if I hadn't held on tightly to their leashes. Both of them believed that it was a dog's mission in life to chase cats up trees and bark their heads off to keep them up there. So I had no previous experience with a dog who actually loved cats with a passion.

According to Dr. Michael Fox, a famous veterinarian and author, dogs don't really hate cats at all. They just pretend that cats are prey, although this attitude doesn't extend to any cats in their own families. Dogs usually get along well with their feline "siblings," but when they see a cat out of doors, they'll stalk it. If the cat runs, and it almost always runs, then it becomes a chase, and a dog loves a good chase. The dog becomes the hunter and the cat the hunted. To the dog, it's only a game, although the cat tends to view it with more of a dubious eye.

Of course, if the cat should stand its ground, and especially if the cat's claws come in contact with the dog's nose, then it's a different story for the dog. According to Dr. Fox, writing in his syndicated newspaper column "Ask the Vet," "Very few dogs will actually attack a cat, and even fewer dogs are cat-killers. A few cats, however, will attack dogs and drive them away."

For his *Newsday* article featuring me and Ginny in the fall of 1995, Matt Villano asked an animal behavior consultant, Dr. Victoria Voith, why she thought Ginny is so attracted to cats. Dr. Voith had a ready answer, although she's never met Ginny or seen her at work. She believed that Ginny's natural attraction may be the result of an overwhelming maternal instinct, and went on to say, "It's not uncommon for females who tend to raise large numbers of young to adopt other offspring as their own. It's just more common for them to adopt infants out of their own species. Ginny is obviously maternally motivated, which means that she'll love anything that will let her."

All dogs are adept at detecting hidden cats, Matt wrote, citing Dr. Voith, and most dogs will be inclined to seek out physically handicapped cats because their instincts tell them that the disabled cats are weaker and easier to approach. "Because Philip is positively responsive to Ginny's behavior, she's made a practice of it," went the doctor's theory. "Philip's love for these strays is basically telling Ginny that it's okay for her to find more and more. They feed on each other."

It sounds like a good theory, and who am I to contradict a behavior specialist? As far as Ginny goes, the one thing I absolutely agree with Dr. Voith about is that Ginny will love anything that will let her. Except for dogs. Ginny does not care for other dogs at all. She never has. Only to one dog did she ever show affection—he was a wonderful Labrador named Coffee.

We told his story in our first book—how Coffee always carried a stick in his mouth like a security blanket and never allowed anyone to touch it, especially not another dog. But Ginny ran up to him without fear, taking the stick into her own mouth, and he let her. Whenever they met, they would play together with that stick, with great affection between them.

The bottom line: Coffee was totally blind, another disabled subject of Ginny's remarkable empathy. I'd like to hear Dr. Voith's theory on that.

We've all seen cute photos in the tabloids showing

mother cats (or dogs) nursing a squirrel or a rabbit or even a mouse along with their own litter. But those animals are at the very height of maternal instinct—their milk is flowing and they have babies at the breast. Their female hormone level at that time is very high.

Not to contradict Dr. Voith, but Ginny is a spay, with a low hormone level. Also, she never raised a lot of puppies because she was only a year old when I took her from the shelter. She had only three puppies. Even so, Ginny actually does seem to believe that she is the mother of all cats everywhere, as well as their guardian and protector.

And, to finish off my first point, what accounts for homeless cats' reactions to Ginny? Sure, *now* they associate her with breakfast and dinner, but those cats trusted Ginny from the very beginning. Even if a cat was particularly timid or paranoid, as soon as my dog did her Ginny Crawl it would respond as though it understood exactly what Ginny was trying to say—that she is no threat. Why, whenever we arrive with the food, do so many of our outdoor cats push one another out of the way to be the one closest to Ginny? They don't act that way about the food. No, the rapport, the empathy between Ginny and cats is unexplainable, even by the most respected animal behavior therapist.

Second, I never encouraged Ginny to begin her cat rescues. On the contrary, I did almost everything I could to *dis*courage her. At the beginning I wasn't particularly fond of cats. I had no "love for strays," as the doctor suggests, and I certainly never wanted a house full of them. This was something Ginny decided all on her own, and she kept dragging reluctant me along with her until she finally made me a convert and an enthusiastic partner and cat-lover.

As for other dogs locating disabled cats, when have you ever heard of any other dog who does what Ginny does—go out twice a day every day with the purpose and determination to save cats' lives? Or any other dog who has effected so many rescues of cats that humans have abandoned as garbage? No, neither have I.

Dr. Lewis J. Gelfand, our veterinarian and president of the All Creatures Veterinary Clinic, where Dr. Carl Darby and Dr. Wayne Geltman work with him, knows Ginny very well, and he agrees with me. "All of Ginny's efforts are concentrated on cats," he says. "Ginny's hormone levels are not high, so it's not a maternal reaction, it's a personality trait. I've never seen or read about anything like it. For a dog to show that kind of instinct toward stray cats is unheard of. She is a unique being.

"It seems to me that Philip and Ginny are very much alike in their dedication to homeless and ill cats. He is the same kind of human that Ginny is a dog, both extremely rare and unique individuals, both with an unbelievable amount of patience and love to give. But whenever we lose a cat—and occasionally we do—Philip takes it very hard. Each and every cat means a great deal to him personally, and he finds it close to impossible to let go.

"At the beginning, we had some real miracles—Topsy and Tulip have endured the most and come back from the most extremes. I had the greatest sense of gratification from them. My pleasure comes from seeing what I have taken them through and what I have brought them to. But they can't all be Topsys and Tulips, so when Sheilah pleads, 'You

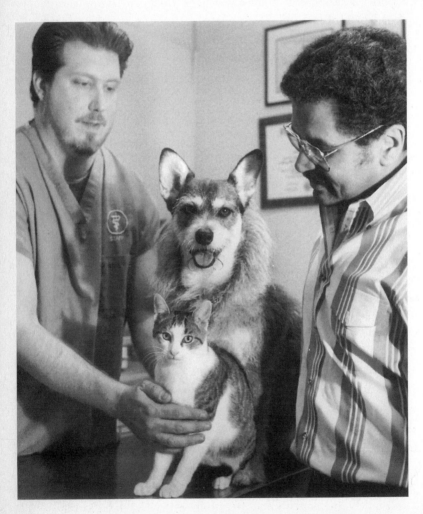

Ginny and the Chairman get clean bills of health from Steve at All Creatures, our veterinary office.

can't give up!' it's often hard to make her and Philip understand and accept that not every sad story can have a happy ending. There's sometimes a limit to what even the most attentive medical care can accomplish.

"To be perfectly fair, Philip views what he does as betterment for the individual cat, whereas I see his work from a medical point of view, as the improvement of the stray cat population at large. By his program of medical treatment, neutering, and inoculation Philip extends the quality of cats' lives, and he also controls the population and disease. Anybody who says he's just attracting more cats to the neighborhood is just wrong. He's actually dead-ending the overpopulation of strays. To me, the key to what Ginny and Philip and Sheilah do is in the numbers."

Explanations of Ginny's behavior continue to flow in from many sources. What *I* believe is that Ginny is a messenger of God's love, a real angel from heaven. That's what I stated in my first book, and nothing has happened since then to change my mind. If anything, I'm even more convinced that Ginny is an angel. It would explain her unique and magical powers. What Sheilah believes is that Ginny must have been a cat herself in an earlier life, which accounts for her incredible empathy with her former species. Sheilah is very spiritual.

GINNY VISITS HER PUBLISHER

Jason Kaufman, our editor on *The Dog Who Rescues Cats*, with the publicists Marshall Trow and Krista Nordgren, came out to visit Ginny and the cats and me in Long Beach one sweltering hot day last summer. They brought lunch for me and a couple of cases of cat food for all our cats. We had a great time together, but I knew that Ginny wanted to go and see her publishing house and meet the rest of the HarperCollins folks. So, in August 1995, Sheilah and I decided to take Ginny into Manhattan to meet Larry Ashmead, a HarperCollins vice president in charge of trade books. Larry is the man who signed up *The Dog Who Rescues Cats*. He always had faith in us and in the book. Then we planned to visit Phyllis Levy and all of Phyllis's fellow editors and friends at *Good Housekeeping*.

This was a giant undertaking. We live out on the Island, and to get into Manhattan we have to take the Long Island Railroad to Penn Station, and then a cab from there. The railroad doesn't permit you to take dogs on the leash onto the train. With the exception of seeing-eye dogs, they all have to be in carriers.

Ginny hated the carrier; it terrified her. When I put her into it, she began to tremble all over and whimper, and her face was so sad it could break your heart. Nothing looks as sad as an unhappy dog with big, sad brown eyes, especially when it's your dog and you love her so much. I think she was afraid that we were taking her somewhere to abandon her. During the train ride, I opened the carrier and put my hand in and stroked Ginny, calling her "good girl" and trying to comfort her. She calmed down a little, but she was still shaking.

We had to change trains at Jamaica, and while we waited on the platform for the next train to arrive, I let Ginny out of her carrier and walked her around a little. This made her feel a lot better, but the miserable look came over her face again when the Manhattan train arrived and she had to go back into her box. When we pulled into Penn Station, we tried to check her carrier so we wouldn't have to drag it along with us, but they only check baggage, so we were stuck with it. Once Ginny was in the taxi with Sheilah and me, though, the trembling and the whimpering stopped cold, and she began to be more like her old self again.

I myself wasn't feeling too well. Since my accident I'm subject to frequent severe headaches, and that day I could feel a migraine headache really building up. I was in pain and nauseated. We got out at the HarperCollins address, a handsome modern building in midtown Manhattan. I had Ginny on the leash, while poor Sheilah was forced to drag the carrier. When we arrived at the security desk before the elevators, we were stopped by the guards. There's a strict policy that animals aren't allowed inside the building, and they were determined to enforce it. There were four or five security guards, and they were all about six feet plus. They kept saying "no" very firmly.

It was beginning to look as though we had come all this way for nothing.

Larry Ashmead's secretary Kathleen, at six feet a young woman who could look the guards in the eye, came down to escort us up, but the guards still said "no way." It seemed to be a standoff. But then (as I found out later) Gene, a long-time HarperCollins executive who knows how to bend rules and regulations, had the bright idea of calling down and telling security that Ginny was a seeing-eye dog and that Philip Gonzalez was blind.

Thanks to the head injuries I suffered in my accident, I can't bear strong light, so I almost always wear sunglasses with really dark lenses whenever I leave my apartment. I had them on, and nobody could look through them and see my eyes, so the guards had to accept the seeing-eye story. Jason came down and escorted us up in the elevator.

On the editorial floor, Larry Ashmead was waiting for us at the elevator. In fact, there was a real welcoming committee; a lot of the HarperCollins people, from all the floors of the company, came out to meet Ginny. When she saw all those people, Ginny knew she had a brand-new audience of hearts to capture. She broke into a large smile, and her tail began to wag like a motor.

It was a real love fest, with tickling, scratching, ear-rubbing, kisses, and young people rolling on the floor with Ginny, who was in seventh heaven. Everyone formed a circle around her and she just kissed every hand and face she could reach. We were told later that more of the HarperCollins people turned out to meet Ginny than had turned out for another author of theirs—Newt Gingrich!

We had named a cat Lucinda for Lucinda Karter, who sold most of the foreign publishing rights to *The Dog Who Rescues Cats*, and now Ginny was able to give her some special one-on-one tail-wagging, face-licking grateful attention.

Larry Ashmead, who is a playful and mischievous man, told Ginny, "Find me a cat, Ginny." He knew very well that there was no cat in any of the offices.

Instantly, Ginny took off. She ran straight to the Xerox

room, where there was a shoeshine machine. Grabbing one of the shoeshine brushes in her teeth, she yanked it off the machine and brought it back to Larry. Well, even he had to admit that the brush was as close to a cat as Ginny could turn up in the HarperCollins offices. At least it was soft and fuzzy, and she chose the black one, not the bright red buffer.

Next, she scampered down the hallway and burst unexpectedly into the office of the publisher, Jack McKeown. There was a high-level meeting going on, and none of the executives gave Ginny a second glance, as though an excited dog racing into an office was an everyday occurrence. If anybody had told them that this was no ordinary dog but one of their best-selling authors (at that time, the hardcover was already into its seventh printing), it might have made a difference in her reception.

Ginny also had her first book-signing. Using a nontoxic stamp pad, she "paw-tographed" books for her new friends. Now she was officially a member of the HarperCollins publishing family. Among her new fans, Lucinda's boss Brenda Segel got one of the "paw-tographed" books. I'd like to add that in these days of fax machines and modems, voice mail and e-mail, some so-called "busy" authors are using high-tech mechanical writers to autograph their books, but Ginny Gonzalez stamped her own paw print with her own paw on the flyleaf of every book.

Thanks to my migraine I missed all of Ginny's cute tricks. I was in the rest room throwing up.

At last it was time to go; we still had to visit Phyllis Levy. Larry called a car service to take us crosstown to *Good Housekeeping*, and he told us the car would wait for us and take us all back to Long Beach. This generous gesture was very good news, because my headache wasn't letting up even a notch, and the thought of the train trip, with changing trains and Ginny miserable and trembling in the carrier, was more than I could deal with.

So we thanked them all, said good-bye, and headed across town.

It took us quite a long while to get from Fifth Avenue (HarperCollins) to Eighth Avenue (*Good Housekeeping*) because they were holding the MTV Music Awards at Radio City Music Hall on Sixth Avenue and many of the streets were blocked off. It was a New York traffic nightmare. At last we made it to Phyllis's office, where Ginny made a whole new group of friends, stopping off in the offices of special people, such as editor-in-chief Ellen Levine, to say hello. She was welcomed by one and all and was very happy.

On the way home, we stopped in Central Park so that I could walk Ginny, but when we got back to the car, Ginny hopped into the front seat and covered the driver with kisses. Sheilah and I sat quietly in the backseat all the way home, happy to have met all the wonderful men and women who had worked so hard to make us a success.

GINNY'S POSSE

Even with all her incredible energy, especially where homeless cats are concerned, my friend Sheilah sometimes gets tired. She'd go to bed between 10:30 and midnight some nights, only to have to drag herself awake again a few hours later to drive me and Ginny to the 4:30 A.M. cat feeding. Then she'd go to work (and she puts in ten-hour days at her computer job), come home, and almost immediately have to go out feeding cats again. No wonder she feels pooped! She's working practically around the clock.

We've made some very good friends thanks to Ginny. Some of them, who knew our story from *Good Housekeeping*, *Newsday*, TV, or my first book, wanted to get involved in helping our strays. Some—Annie Visceglia, Terry Dunbar, and Marilyn Sainthill—volunteered to help us feed cats by taking over some of Sheilah's driving chores.

Annie's mother, Regina Visceglia, goes shopping for our cat food. Her nephew, Chris Carter (*not* the "X-Files" director) is thirteen years old, and he loves helping me in my work. He recently bought us a case of cat food with his own money, and he promises that, when he's old enough to get his driver's license, he'll take me around to feed our cats, even though he's allergic to them and has to take Benadryl. I'm allergic, too, and I take Proventil in an inhaler.

Whenever I have to go somewhere suddenly, Carole Feldman and Laurie Marrone will happily baby-sit Ginny for me. Ruby Leivent answers my mail and writes thank-you notes when it is difficult for me to write with only my left hand. And Diane Bell writes to various cat food companies, soliciting donations of food for our outside cats. She is often successful, and every free mouthful helps, because we always seem to be feeding more and more cats. I think of our wonderful crew of volunteers as "Ginny's posse."

❖   ❖   ❖

Ginny's "mommy" Sheilah is the Chairman's mommy, too.

Thanks to the help of our wonderful volunteers, Sheilah gets occasional evenings off, which is time she really deserves.

Marilyn Sainthill's mother and father, Herb and Dorothy Rothfuss, have taken in one of our outdoor cats, Molly G., and are fostering her. They recently lost their own cat, who lived with them for twenty years, and wanted to help our rescue effort out. They knew that it costs us nine dollars a day for each outdoor cat to be waiting at the veterinarian's office to be adopted. So they are giving Molly G. a free roof over her head, good food, and love, but she is still up for a permanent home.

Mookie was a cat who belonged to someone who couldn't keep him; one of our volunteer drivers, Terry Dunbar, then adopted him and brought him home to her four other cats and two dogs. He's a handsome five-year-old tabby with a white belly, a great cat. Sheilah was very sorry to see him go; she fell in love with Mookie as soon as she saw him, and felt depressed when the Dunbars picked him up. She was so sad that Terry relented and returned Mookie. Now the lucky little cat has three mothers—Sheilah, Terry, and Ginny. My dog and I visit Sheilah's apartment every day to see our "other" cats, and Mookie is always beside himself with joy when we come in.

Another cat who had that reaction to us was Ruby, the outdoor cat who gave her name to the Ruby's feeding station. Whenever she saw us coming, she would throw herself on the ground and roll around, begging to be picked up. Ruby was a cat who'd already been spayed, and was at All Creatures for six weeks, hoping for a home which she never got. So we had to put her back out on the street. She loved being indoors, and she especially wanted to be with Ginny, Sheilah, and me. Ruby was far more interested in us than in the food we brought. Well, how long could we resist that? Ruby is now an indoor cat, staying with Sheilah, and she still rolls around to get attention and cuddles, but now she rolls on carpeting, and she gets picked up and hugged at least two dozen times a day.

I only wish we could bring all our outdoor cats inside and make them indoor cats. Someday, maybe, when our ship comes in and we build our own shelter, we can invite all our street cats into warmth and light.

Long Island Pet Expo 1995

Ginny and I were invited to be special guests at the Long Beach Humane Society's exhibit at the Long Island Pet Expo in the Nassau Coliseum. We were going to sell and autograph our book for the benefit of the Humane Society. The Expo was held on Sunday, November 17, 1995. Sheilah drove us there, but she didn't want to come in. She told me she'd like to have a day off for herself, without any animals, and she handed me her cellular phone so we could stay in touch. Sheilah promised to come back to the Coliseum later and take Ginny and me home.

We got there about eleven in the morning, and the Expo was already in full swing. As soon as we entered the Coliseum, Ginny's ears stood up straight and tall and her nose began to twitch in excitement. Her tail was going sixty miles an hour. She could see little children taking rides on ponies, and many different animals—birds, lizards, fish, dogs, and cats. She didn't know where to look or sniff first.

We made our way through the crowds to the Long Beach Humane Society's booth, where we met Kenny Colon, and where a table had been set up for Ginny and me to "paw-tograph" *The Dog Who Rescues Cats*. This was actually our first book-signing, and I was a little nervous, hoping that we wouldn't be entirely ignored. It's humiliating to just sit there hopefully while people pass you by without a second look.

No chance of that! Adults and children crowded around us, all of them wanting to meet Ginny, and some of them even wanting to meet me. They recognized Ginny from the *Newsday* article and the two pieces in *Good Housekeeping*. The children were petting Ginny and even hugging her, and my dog was all smiles and ecstatic tail-wags. We made a lot of sales with her paw print as autograph; everyone wanted to say hello to the miraculous dog who saves the lives of home-less cats. Even dealers from other booths came to meet her. And that's when we met Dr. Jonathan Greenfield, whose cable TV program "The Family Pet" is on Channel 12 New York. He came over from his own exhibit to meet her and invited us to do his show. Photographers who had booths at the Expo offered to take Ginny's photograph for free. Ginny was the hit of the Expo.

The same question was asked over and over: How is it that Ginny can find injured cats and kittens? I had to answer honestly, as I always do. I don't know; I can't explain it.

Everybody seemed to have a theory. Maybe Ginny smells blood from the injured animals. Maybe, but not all of

Ginny's rescues were bleeding. Maybe she could hear the cats with her keen sense of hearing. I'm sure that's true, but even the keenest hearing can't penetrate building walls, and remember that Ginny rescued five newborn kittens from a huge pipe inside a building. She sensed their presence from way out in the street. There's more there than just sharp ears.

Maybe God was guiding her to the cats and kittens, somebody said, and I had to agree. It's what I myself believe. Someone else said that Ginny was just simply a hero, and that her miraculous finds were meant to be. Again, I agreed. That's also what I believe. I told them that Ginny has a very special radar of the heart that sets her apart from every other dog in the world.

We were having a wonderful time. Every now and then Kenny would take Ginny out for a walk while I signed books that already had her paw print. At the booth, the Long Beach Humane Society had a group of cats and dogs for adoption, along with a rabbit. Ginny really wanted that rabbit. As soon as she laid eyes on it, she started up her "Gimme . . . gimme . . . " whimper and I just closed my eyes and prayed hard.

My prayers were answered. Another family adopted the rabbit; all the cats and some of the dogs found homes, too. What a relief!

I took Ginny for a stroll around the Coliseum, and she was fascinated by all the different animals she saw. The Expo was beginning to wind down, and the booths were being packed up. But before we left, Art Ackerman from the Long Island Cat Fanciers Association came to meet

Ginny and shake her paw. Always the superstar, Ginny flirted with Art and enchanted him.

I was expecting to hear from Sheilah about when she was coming to pick me up, but when the cellular phone rang, it was Sheilah with a very different message. She could hardly talk. Breathlessly, she told me that while she was driving, a cat had flown right through the air and landed on the hood of her Camry, and could we please get home right away?

I thought Sheilah was kidding me, and I told her so, but Kenny agreed to drive me home. I live just across the courtyard from Sheilah. Now I'm going to let Sheilah continue this story in her own words.

Sheila's Day Off Without Animals

"Did you ever have a day when you just didn't want to do something you normally love to do? A day when you simply want to shirk your duties and break out of your usual routine? That's how I felt on Pet Expo Day.

"'Just give me one day without animals,' I begged Philip. 'You don't really need me there.' And he agreed, although he seemed surprised.

"So after I dropped Philip and Ginny off at the Coliseum, I had a day all to myself, with no responsibilities. I did some personal errands, went to the Laundromat and the dry cleaner, then drove to see a girlfriend I hadn't visited in a long while. We had a good, long talk and then I started driving home. As I drove, I saw a cat running across the parkway and, to my great horror, I thought I saw it disap-

Ken Colon (right) shows Ginny some pit bull puppies, but Ginny wants no part of them. I'm pulling on her leash, but Ginny says, "Forget it!"

pear under the wheels of the car just ahead of me. I uttered a scream and put my foot on the brake, but within the next split second something very bizarre happened.

"Somehow, I didn't understand how, the cat flipped through the air as if it were doing a somersault and landed smack on the hood of my car, where it lay, barely moving. For a moment I sat there on the parkway in shock, then very slowly I pulled over to the shoulder of the road and stopped the car, went out, and examined the hit-and-run victim.

"The cat was injured, bleeding, but alive. And her back legs were still moving, even though she was lying on her side. They were running, running, like a tin toy that has fallen over but hasn't yet wound down.

"My Toyota Camry functions like a combination cat feeder/shelter/ambulance/first-aid station on wheels, and I always have emergency supplies with me. I had some clean laundry from the Laundromat in a basket on the backseat, so I dumped it out quickly, lined the basket with one of the plastic bags I always carry, and went to get the cat.

"I didn't have gloves with me, and I was afraid to touch her with my bare hands; she might be carrying some contagious feline disease that I could transport back to my other cats. Also, I didn't know whether she might strike out at me with teeth or claws because of her terror and pain. Just as important, I didn't want to move her too abruptly in case she had internal injuries. So I took my newspaper and slid it under the cat. Then, using the newspaper like a hospital gurney, I kind of scraped her off the hood and placed her very gently into the basket. She didn't fight or move, and I drove like crazy back to my place.

"Philip and Ginny were still at Pet Expo with Ken Colon from the animal shelter. I couldn't take the risk of bringing the poor thing into my apartment because of my other cats; neither Philip nor I bring in any new cats to our homes until they've been cleared by the vet for infectious diseases and had all their shots. So I warmed some towels in the oven and wrapped them around the pathetic victim in her basket to keep her warm. She was still bleeding, and purring like mad, but I know that cats purr not only when they are happy but also when they're afraid or when they're in pain.

"As soon as I got the little cat tucked in, I phoned Philip. I had lent him my cellular phone to carry with him, so reaching him at the Expo was no problem. When I described what happened, and how the cat flipped up through the air, landing on my hood, Philip laughed at me.

"'No way could that happen. What, was it raining cats and dogs outside?' And he laughed again at his own little joke.

"But I knew that not only *could* it, it *did* happen exactly that way. Still, I wasn't going to waste my breath arguing; time enough when Philip came back with Ginny and Ken and we could get the hurt animal to Dr. Gelfand's office. So I asked Philip to come back as soon as possible.

"When the guys returned home, they came right over to see my 'mythical' cat, and were totally surprised to find her real. We took her in the basket to the veterinarian.

"The cat's pelvis was broken and, when Dr. Gelfand began surgery, he discovered that one of her back legs was shattered. A rod in her leg and a pin in her hip were the best chance she would have to recover fully or almost fully.

As expensive as these procedures were, we authorized them. We couldn't and wouldn't do otherwise.

"But there, too, this little cat seemed to have nine lives. Maxine Beige, a wonderful woman who had read about us in *Newsday* and has a dog and eight cats of her own, sent a generous gift for Philip to use for our rescues, and it took care not only of Sue's surgery (we named the accident victim after an assistant of Dr. Gelfand's) but of several other cats who were having medical treatments at the same time. So, for a change, money was not a problem this time. (We named two cats for Ms. Beige, Maxine and Beige, and she was very pleased when both of them found homes.)

"And this I just have to tell you. Dr. Gelfand informed Philip and Kenny that my story of the cat somersaulting through the air to land on my hood must be absolutely true, because Sue's injuries were in line with that scenario. He even demonstrated how it could happen, and how Sue had managed to avoid getting run over. She was struck hard by the car's front bumper, which ricocheted her like a pool ball, straight up in the air and backward, so she hadn't actually fallen under the wheels of the car that hit her.

"But the story doesn't end there. While Sue was recovering from her surgery, a man saw her in the vet's office and fell for her, even though she was still a mess. He would visit her a couple of times a week, riding to the office on his bicycle. He was interested in taking Sue home, but first he wanted to be certain that she'd make an affectionate pet. After all, she'd been running wild in the streets and the parkway.

"Well, Sue and this man bonded, and the more he visited her the more affectionate the two of them became.

"On Christmas Eve, almost two months after Sue entered the hospital, she went home with her new owner. At the same time, Bad Mike and Sweet Pea also found homes—three Christmas Eve adoptions. When we went to the Blessing of the Animals that evening, we were already exhilarated by this special Christmas gift.

"Since then, I've often thought about 'Sheilah's Day Off Without Animals.' Why that day of all days did I decide to break free and go my own way? What if I hadn't? What if I'd gone along to the Pet Expo? If I hadn't been on the parkway when Sue was hit by the car, she would not have survived. I'm convinced of that. She would have lain on the road until the next set of wheels drove over her, snuffing out her young life. Instead, she's just about as good as new and has an infinitely better quality of life, enjoying love and kindness and a permanent home. Sue's troubles are behind her now; her future looks bright, and will be spent in peace and affection.

"If you want to know what I think, I think some of Ginny's own personal magic rubbed off on me that day. And it must have rubbed off on Sue as well, saving eight of her nine lives. Not to mention that it taught me a lesson. I learned that for Sheilah Harris, there *is* no 'day off without animals.' And that's okay with me."

RAINBOW BRIDGE

As every animal lover knows, unless you own a tortoise or an elephant, our pets' life spans are far, far too short. A cat can live way up into its twenties—if it's got good genes and good luck—but even that is not long enough for the human owner who has loved that cat for more than twenty years. Dogs usually don't even live that long, and big dogs are lucky to see ten years. This is a bitter regret all of us who love animals feel. Too bad we can't aim our remote controls at our precious pets and rewind them like videotapes, back to their kittenhood and puppyhood. If love could keep our pets alive, they'd every one of them be immortal.

Recently, a friend sent me a little fable that came in over the Internet, right out of cyberspace, where it has been circulating. No name was attached to it in authorship, which is too bad, because I'd love to give the right person credit for it (I'd also love to take credit for it myself, but I can't). I want to share this with you anyway.

Just this side of heaven is a place called Rainbow Bridge. When an animal dies that has been especially close to someone here, that pet goes to Rainbow Bridge. There are meadows and hills for all of our special friends so they can run and play together. There is plenty of food and water and sunshine, and our friends are warm and comfortable. All the animals who had been ill and old are restored to health and vigor; those who were hurt and maimed are made whole and strong again, just as we remember them in our dreams of days and times gone by.

The animals are happy and content, except for one small thing: They miss someone very special to them, someone who had to be left behind.

They spend their time in play together, but the day finally comes when one animal suddenly stops and looks into the distance. The bright eyes are intent; the eager body quivers. Suddenly he or she begins to break away from the group, almost flying over the green grass. Four legs carry him faster and faster. YOU have been spotted, and when you and your special friend finally meet, you cling together in a joyous reunion, never again to be parted from each other. The happy kisses rain damply on your face, your hands caress again the beloved head and body, and you look once more into the trusting eyes of your pet, so long gone from your life, but never for one day absent from your heart.

Then you cross Rainbow Bridge together.

I think that's a beautiful possibility, and I can see the same thing happening to me in the future, many years from now, I hope. I'll bet that when Vinola passed over, there was a mighty thundering of cat paws in her direction. But it will be just a bit different in my case. When Ginny and I are spotted (and yes, she has promised to stay with me forever, so we're not going unless we go together), there will come scampering toward us a giant herd of cats, hundreds and hundreds and hundreds of cats, indoor cats and outdoor cats, all of whom have been loved and cared for by us. The sound of purring will be deafening as they get closer to Ginny and Philip, with Montoose and Husky barking happily in the rear as the cats push them out of the way to get to us first.

And, on Rainbow Bridge, none of them will be blind or lame or deaf or brain-damaged or missing limbs or feet. Betty Boop will have back paws, Jackie and Revlon will see perfectly out of two good eyes, Madame will hear a pin drop a couple of rooms away, and Topsy will stand up and run straight and strong. None will have feline leukemia or AIDS and none will be abused or starving or lost or lonely. There will be plenty of kittens, because there will be enough loving laps to hold them all when we cross over Rainbow Bridge.

If only we could make Earth itself into Rainbow Bridge during our lifetimes, what a world this would be!